Michigan Haunts and Hauntings

Dedicated to my granddaughters,
Krystal, Ashley, Corinne, and Rya.

May they always enjoy hearing and telling a good tale.

The third printing of Michigan Haunts and Hauntings
is dedicated to the memory of Marion Kuclo,
The Green Witch Gundella
(1930-1993)

Michigan Haunts and Hauntings

Marion Kuclo
The Green Witch Gundella

Thunder Bay Press
Lansing, Michigan

Manufactured in the United States of America

1996 1997   8 7 6 5 4

Illustrations by Christopher Petersen.
Cover design by Rachel Levenberg, SunGraphics
Edited by Frances King Koch.

Thunder Bay Press

Lansing, Michigan

ISBN 1-882376-00-5

CONTENTS

Contents continued

Foreword

Marion Kuclo, best known to her admiring Michigan audiences as the witch "Gundella," has been avidly collecting supernatural tales and ghostlore for more than forty years. For some twenty-five of those years, I have had the pleasure of knowing this warm and generous lady and am among the many she has has enchanted with her personality and her energy for life and all its mysteries.

Gundella has lived in lower Michigan since 1948. As a school teacher for many years, she acquired a well-earned reputation for her dramatic story-telling at children's assemblies. A popular Detroit area lecturer and prominent media personality, she has known most of the local and visiting figures from the Occult World. Through her many public workshops and lectures, television and radio appearances, and her regular newspaper column, Gundella has come to know a remarkable range of people. And through her talent for listening, she has gathered an enormous amount of our local lore. She has also been in the unique position of learning about this area's strange events from those who sought her help in exorcising spirits and otherwise dealing with the paranormal.

Those who recall Gundella's first collection *The Werewolf of Grosse Pointe and Other Stories* (which quickly sold out of its small 1976 printing and is now a collector's item) will especially welcome this new collection. Not only is it more extensive in its range and coverage, but it again reflects the diligence and careful research Gundella's readers have come to know. In this new volume, she goes well beyond simply providing us with an oral history of this region's tales of wonder. She has carefully researched each of these stories, visiting their sites and interviewing witnesses wherever possible. This has enabled her to unearth many obscure and often fascinating details about Michigan lore that otherwise might be lost to us. Aside from being entertaining, these tales of haunts and hauntings are an important contribution to the record of our local cultural heritage.

Gundella brings special authority to her studies. A traditional witch, she is part of a family whose background in witchcraft (what some call the Old Religion) extends back several generations. Initiated into a coven as a young girl in upstate Michigan, she can trace her family roots back to the Green Witches of Scotland. (She tells us that green dye was chosen by her ancestors to camouflage their bodies for secret travel through the woods for coven meetings.)

Gundella is certainly not alone in her preoccupation with "things that go bump in the night." A 1990 Gallup poll indicated that some 93% of all Americans believe in at least one form of supernatural, psychic, paranormal or otherwise "otherworldly" phenomenon. We in Michigan are no exception. And Gundella shows us a wealth of evidence that Michigan abounds with tales of such wonders. Whether you read her stories as real proof of the supernatural or simply as wonderful examples of modern mythology, this volume will give you one of the liveliest and most romantic perspectives on Michigan that you're likely to find anywhere.

Marcello Truzzi, Ph.D.
Eastern Michigan University

Preface

I am a witch. I am also a very ordinary person and I live in an ordinary house in an ordinary community. I spent more than 20 years of my life teaching school and I now have children and grandchildren of my own. Some people are actually disappointed to learn that I am not a little weirder. They want their witches to have bats hanging upsidedown in the corners and cauldrons boiling over an open fire.

I became involved in witchcraft in a very normal way: I was born into a family where it was practiced. My mother, grandmother, and great-grandmother were witches, and so were many of my other relatives. They claim that we can trace our involvement in the craft back to the Green Witches of Scotland who practiced during the Middle Ages.

Back then, in Western Europe and the British Isles, there were three cults of witches: the red, the blue, and the green. Blue witches were primarily interested in the heavens and studied astronomy and astrology; red witches were alchemists; and green witches were agricultural people who dealt with herbs and teas, and the treatments and potions made from them. These witches frequently anointed their skins with vegetable dyes that identified them with their particular cult, much as American Indians did when they painted their faces with certain designs that identified their individual tribes. My family descended from the green witches of Scotland, and I occasionally dye my skin with green food coloring when I present a folklore program. It's my way of illustrating a long abandoned practice.

My heritage did not automatically make me a witch. But if you're born into a family of Lutherans you are far more likely to grow up a Lutheran than you are a Baptist or a Catholic. When I was old enough to decide for myself, I chose to become a witch. I was initiated into a traditional coven in Ann Arbor, Michigan, in 1948 when I was 18.

I'd tell you more about witchcraft, but that's not what this book is about. This book is about ghosts, and as a witch I was taught not to fear ghosts, but to try to accept and understand them.

Do you believe in ghosts? Most people do, even those who don't acknowledge it. If you believe in a separable soul, or you feel that when you die a part of you lives on in some way, then, my friend, you DO believe in ghosts.

The question is not whether ghosts exist, but whether these disembodied spirits can communicate with those of us who still inhabit earthly bodies of flesh and blood. I believe they can and do, and for that reason I have put together this collection of assorted ghostly tales, all of which involve people and places in Michigan. Many of these stories are about people I am acquainted with, and some others have been told to me by sane, intelligent individuals who I believe to be completely serious and sincere. Some, such as the North American Indian legends and a few of the older stories are from my personal folklore collection begun while I was in high school. And many of the more modern tales (especially in Parts X through XIII) come straight from the front pages of local Michigan newspapers.

I cannot prove the authenticity of any of these ghosts. Ghosts do not take well to following rules or conforming to the controls necessary for true scientific discovery. However, I have investigated the particular events disclosed here to the best of my ability. In some cases, I have become quite involved with them. Minnie Quay (in Part XIII), for instance, has become as real to me as my own great-grandmother who lived in the same time period and in the same part of Michigan. I have spent a great deal of time over the last five years visiting Minnie's house, becoming familiar with her home town and the surrounding area, and getting to know the surviving descendants of her brothers and sisters.

I hope you will find the hauntings described here as enthralling as I have. Some may inspire you to visit their locations and do a bit of research on your own. For this reason, I've provided a map at the back of the book which could prove useful.

Whenever possible, in these pages, I've used real names. In a few

cases, I have respected the wishes of those involved and used fictitious names or first names only to protect their privacy.

Any good story, and especially one about ghosts, becomes even
better when shared. Try reading these tales aloud around an open
fire or at least by candlelight. Once the right mood is set, you may be
surprised to discover how readily others will share their own ghostly
encounters.

Gundella

I

North American Indian Legends

Long ago the pagan peoples of Western Europe and the British Isles believed that in the fall of each year the earth died, and that after lying dormant through the long, cold winter months, it was reborn each spring. October 31, All Hallow's Eve, which is roughly halfway between the autumnal equinox and the winter solstice, was not only a witches' sabbath, but the date on which special rituals were conducted by others to communicate with the dead. The ancient Greeks and Romans maintained that the souls of the departed were most likely to revisit the earth at that time, and performed traditional ceremonies to commemorate them. When the early Christian church sought to convert certain of these peoples to Catholicism, it found them unwilling to part with their old ways. So, the church established All Saints Day on November 1, observed as a Christian feast day to honor the saints, and All Souls Day, November 2, as a day of prayer for the souls of all others departed. Strange as it may seem, halfway around the world, on a continent Europeans had yet to discover, North American Indians were also practicing similar rituals at the same time of year to communicate with their dead. Annually, when the leaves fell, ghost dances were performed to call up the spirits of their departed ancestors. Early American explorers and settlers found that Indian folklore was rich with stories about ghosts. Here are a few of my favorites that are said to have taken place right in the state of Michigan.

The Snake Goddess of Bell Isle and The Oracle of Peach Island

(an Ottawa Indian Legend)

Chief Sleeping Bear had a daughter so beautiful that he kept her in a covered boat moored in the Detroit River to keep her from being ogled by ordinary men.

One day, as her father was visiting to bring her food, the girl was seen by the winds that blew along the river. They were so taken by her beauty they could not contain themselves, and they began to huff and puff, trying to remove the cover from her boat so that they could gaze upon her at will. So fiercely did the winds blow that the moorings snapped and the little craft floated away down the river.

As the boat passed by the lodge of the keeper of the water-gates, its protective cover flew off and the maiden was exposed to view. Awed by her great beauty, the lodgekeeper pursued the boat and brought the girl ashore. But as he carried her into his wigwam, the angry winds fell upon him, buffeting him wildly about until he finally died of the beating.

Now sorry for what they had done, the winds returned the maiden unharmed to the home of her father. They begged the Indian chief not to hide her from them again, but to let them see her and enjoy her beauty. Chief Sleeping Bear agreed to this, but he lived in fear that some mortal man would again try to carry her off. To protect her, he placed the girl on an island in the Detroit River and prevailed upon the Great Spirit to surround the island with snakes to protect her from intruders. There she could run free with the winds around her. The snakes were so charmed by her unmatched beauty that they began to worship her. Seeing this, the Great Spirit made her immortal, to dwell upon the island and rule over it for eternity.

When the first white men appeared in the area they named the island Isle Ste. Clair. As they became familiar with it, they renamed it Rattlesnake Island. It was not until much later that it became known by its present name, Belle Isle.

To this day, the maiden's spirit can be seen from time to time dancing in the wind on the island. Most unsuspecting picnickers don't realize that the lovely girl in Indian costume is not a modern miss dressed for some pageant, but is in reality the Goddess of Belle Isle.

Her erstwhile suitor, the water-gate keeper who had been killed by the angry winds was buried on Isle au Peche (Peach Island) where his spirit remained for generations. Indian braves sought out this spirit for counsel before going into battle. His voice sounded like wind among the trees and could be understood only by those who had prepared themselves through fasting and meditation.

Before planning his campaign against the English, Chief Pontiac spent seven days on Isle au Peche, fasting in order to "clear his ear" to seek the wisdom of the Oracle of Peach Island.

The Wailing Maidens of the Sister Isles

Long ago on the banks of the Detroit River, where the city of Wyandotte now stands, there lived a Wyandot chief who had three beautiful daughters. Although they were lovely to look at, these girls were quarrelsome creatures whose constant bickering made them unbearable company.

None of the young braves of the village wanted to marry them. Their reputations even spread to neighboring tribes, and it became impossible for the old chief to find husbands for them. They were so difficult to get along with that even the other women avoided them. The old chief had moved his daughters to separate wigwams far apart from the rest of the tribe, but even there, they quarreled among themselves so loudly and so long that they disturbed the entire community.

Their scolding and wrangling continued until finally the chief could stand it no more. He separated them even from each other, placing them on each of three islands to keep them apart. These islands, in western Lake Erie, came to be known as the Sister Isles. When the sisters could no longer argue and quarrel with each other, they began to scream and cry. They neither ate nor slept, and continued their sobbing and crying until all three finally wasted away.

Some say their wailing can still be heard by sailors aboard the freighters that pass by these islands. Others insist that it is only the wind they hear. To this day, the islands remain uninhabited and no one seems to want to go near them.

The Folly of Father Dollier and Father Galinee

When LaSalle set out to find the Ohio River, of which he had heard the Indians speak, he took with him two French Catholic priests, Father Dollier and Father Galinee, whose intention was to establish a Christian mission among the Indians.

Near the site of what is now Hamilton, Ontario, on September 24, 1669, they met a seasoned explorer named Adrien Jolliet who, with Ottawa Indians as his guides, had traveled south along the Michigan shore of Lake Huron, through the St. Clair River, the Detroit River, and the north shore of Lake Erie. Jolliet talked with the Fathers and drew them a map of the waters he had traveled. He urged them to follow his route, and assured them that in that area there were many tribes to whom they might carry the Christian religion. The priests then left LaSalle's party and traveled north, following Jolliet's map.

On the Michigan side of the Detroit River, near what is now the site of the Detroit Renaissance Center, they found an Indian shrine. Here the Ottawas worshipped at a natural stone formation on which they had painted a face. To the Indians, it was a sacred place where they would bring their offerings of furs, foods, and tobacco to Manitou (their name for the Great Spirit the white men called God).

Determined that the Indians should no longer worship false gods and stone idols, Father Galinee overturned the rock and smashed it to bits. The largest piece fell into the river. Then, in order to leave no trace of the idol, the two Fathers loaded the smaller stone pieces into their canoe and carried them out into the deeper part of the river, where they threw them overboard.

The Indians who had assembled on shore watched dumbstruck at the audacity of the white men. The Great Spirit spoke to them and told them to retrieve the large piece which had fallen into the river and take it out to where the priests had discarded the smaller pieces. When they had done this, all of the rock pieces joined together and became a monster serpent that protected the place from further intrusion.

Ten years later, in 1679 when LaSalle ascended the straits in his ship called Griffin, the Indians invoked the help of Manitou. Strange forms rose up from the waters and pushed the ship north through Lake St. Clair, the St. Clair River, and into Lake Huron where it was whipped about by a ferocious storm. Finally, the sturdy little ship reached St. Ignace, or Michilimackinaw as the Indians called it. There, LaSalle and his crew rested for several days before sailing on to Green Bay.

After loading the ship with furs, LaSalle ordered the captain to take the ship back to Niagara, while he continued on his way along the western coast of Lake Michigan by canoe. All went well with the Griffin until she again entered the waters of Lake Huron. No one really knows what happened after that, but the little ship was never seen or heard from again. The Indians believed that the water spirits conjured up to protect them from the intrusion of the white man had lain in wait in Lake Huron for the Griffin to return. When she did, they drove her relentlessly to her destruction.

II

The Haunted Past

The stories included here are all well over 100 years old, and are about some of the first people to live in Michigan, and — more importantly—some of the first ghosts to haunt here. With the exception of the first, "The One Hundredth Skull," these stories are from old private collections. Some were first written down in French and later translated into English, while others were passed down from storyteller to storyteller for decades before being written down. In 1961 I was teaching school in South Rockwood when I met a young man named Jim Quick from Monroe. We shared an interest in Michigan folklore and especially in the collecting and telling of ghost stories. Jim was then teaching sixth grade in the Airport Community School District. He went on to become an English instructor at the University of Michigan, and in 1965 when I last heard of him, he was preparing to leave for Hollywood to become a script writer. "The One Hundredth Skull" had been passed down through his family as a tale about some of his own relatives who had been among the very early settlers along what is now the Michigan-Ohio border.

The One Hundredth Skull

In the late 1700s, a frontiersman named Bill Quick lived with his aged father in a log cabin a few miles west of Lake Erie. One day while he was out hunting, his cabin was ransacked and his father was murdered and scalped. Bill swore he would not rest until he had taken revenge one hundred times over. He set himself a secret goal: he would kill 100 Indians before he died.

Never a sociable man to begin with, Bill kept even more to himself after his father's murder. And because he was an excellent marksman, he had little trouble in the first few years working toward his goal. He did not collect scalps like most men of that time and place; scalps were not enough for him. Bill Quick collected skulls. He lined his walls with shelves to hold his ghastly trophies, and one by one, his collection grew.

Year after year he relentlessly stalked his prey. He took his time, always waiting patiently until he saw a lone figure hunting in the woods or paddling a canoe on the river. Only when there was no one else about would his bullet zing through the air and into an Indian heart. The Indians were unable to retaliate because they never knew who was picking them off one at a time. So, as the years went by, fewer and fewer of them traveled alone in that area.

His game became more difficult to obtain as the Indians became more cautious, but Bill finally amassed 99 grizzly skulls. They stood in a row on the shelves of his innocent looking log house deep in the woods. He felt certain he would have no difficulty meeting his ultimate goal — certain that he could easily shoot the one remaining Indian needed to complete his revenge. But, before he had the satisfaction of making his one last kill, Bill Quick fell victim to what he knew would be his last illness. He summoned his only son, Tom, to his bedside.

The two men had never been close. They had had little or nothing in common. Bill was a fearless hunter with a vicious temper and a cruel sense of humor. Although he enjoyed his whiskey, he did not drink to excess and no one could ever remember seeing him drunk. He never went about without his rifle and never had to shoot twice at the same target. Tom, on the other hand, was an easygoing fellow who never bore a grudge. Although he enjoyed fishing, Tom disliked hunting and had never learned to shoot well. He didn't even own a gun, a rarity in those times. He was seldom sober, but he was a happy drunk and was often heard singing to himself as he stumbled home from the tavern. His mother had died giving birth to him and he had been raised by his maternal grandmother. Never in his life had his father even spoken a pleasant word to him.

Because he knew that his father had always considered him worthless, Tom was more than a little surprised that the old man wanted to see him, even on his deathbed. But he didn't hesitate, and went at once to his father's cabin.

For the first time, Bill confided in Tom, telling him the story of the oath he had taken and the goal he had set. Pointing to the skulls grinning down at them, he demanded that his son fulfill the oath by obtaining the one hundredth skull. The morbid collection caused Tom to retch. As much as he longed for his father's approval, he flatly refused to carry out the macabre order.

But Bill would not let him go. He threatened that if Tom did not do as he asked, he would return from the grave and haunt him until he did. Tom ran screaming from the cabin, the taste of bile rising in his throat. Soon after, his father died and Tom tried to forget the threat by losing himself in drink. But he was no longer a happy drunk. Wherever he looked, he thought he saw his father glaring at him. For the next two years his life was a nightmare.

Then one day, in a drunken stupor, he babbled the gruesome tale and soon people for miles around knew that the town drunk was under oath to kill an Indian. He became a laughing stock and the butt of cruel jokes. Every time an Indian came into town people would make sure Tom knew. They would tease him, telling him to get a gun or offering to lend him theirs. Their taunting echoed after him down the streets where little children would call out "Sic 'em Tom!" as he passed by.

One clear, cold night in October when Tom was alone in his cabin, the door suddenly burst open and there stood the rotting corpse of his father. As he had promised, Bill had returned from the grave to haunt his son. And as he had always done in life, he carried his rifle. Shaking it in the air, he screamed wildly for Tom to go out and get the one hundredth skull so that his ancestors could rest in their graves. He said that if Tom could not complete the task by midnight the next night he would return and bring Tom's murdered grandfather with him.

Tom rushed into town begging for asylum, telling everyone he met about his father's ghostly threat. It was clear to all who saw him that Tom had now gone mad. Everyone, even those who had earlier taunted him, now steered clear of him.

Throughout the following day, Tom searched in vain for someone, anyone, who would help him. As dusk fell, he was last seen stumbling down the old road toward his father's isolated cabin deep in the woods. It had remained undisturbed since Bill Quick's death more than two years earlier. When he did not return by late afternoon the following day, a group of men decided to search for the unfortunate derelict, expecting to find him dead somewhere. When they reached Bill Quick's cabin, they found the door standing open. Cautiously pushing it open, they searched the room. Tom's body was nowhere to be found. Instead, there on the shelf so long reserved for the one hundredth skull was a freshly severed head. But it was not the face of an Indian that stared down at them.

It was the face of the town drunk, Tom Quick.

The Old Lodger

In the mid–1800s, city dwellers often spent their evenings visiting with neighbors. A good storyteller was always popular and the old lodger of the story that follows proved to be an exceptional teller of tales with a seemingly endless repertoire of ghost stories. Charles Skinner was just a child at the time, but he was so fascinated by her stories that well into adulthood he still remembered them well. Eventually, he wrote down several of the tales for posterity. But more spine tingling is the story Mr. Skinner records not by the old lodger, but about her.

Marie Thebault — or Kennette — was a childless widow who made shoes for a living. She owned a two-story house on Old River Road (now Jefferson Avenue) in Detroit that served as both her residence and her place of business. In 1865, she decided to take in a lodger to augment her meager income and rented a room to an elderly French woman whose name has long been forgotten.

Kennette was not very well liked. She was a rude, insensitive person with nothing much good to say about anybody. She seemed to resent her boarder's popularity in the neighborhood and would mock, taunt, and laugh at the gentle, pious old French woman.

Kennette was not a churchgoer. She often expounded at length about her own belief that there was no God, no life after death, no heaven or hell, and above all, no ghosts. She called the old lodger and anyone who listened to her tales a pitiful fool. She loudly boasted that if the old woman died and actually came back to haunt her, then and only then would she change her beliefs. She went so far as to promise that she would even join the church. A bargain was made to that effect between the two women, but Kennette continued to make fun of the old storyteller, who was loved and respected by everyone else.

Finally, death came to the elderly lodger. And while Kennette was discussing the death with a neighbor, the neighbor's son came into the house and — knowing Kennette's miserly ways — asked why she had left a light burning in her house. Kennette, surprised, grabbed a poker and set out to teach her intruder a lesson, for she knew she herself had left no light burning. But when she arrived home, there was no intruder. And no light.

On several evenings after that, as Kennette gadded about the neighborhood, others would report seeing a light burning in her house. But each time she returned home, she always found the house dark.

One evening she decided she would see for herself. She left home as usual, but returned after only a few moments and quietly went in the back door. Creeping to her room, she laid down upon the bed. She had hardly settled herself when she saw a light coming up the stairs.

Kennette bolted up and stood waiting. The light continued soundlessly up the stairs, entered the room, and stopped directly before her. It was not a lantern or a candle, but a white phosphorescence. Its form changed gradually until she could see the cloudy shape of a human being. For the first time in her life Kennette was terrified.

"Come no nearer," she cried. "I know you. I believe you. I was wrong and you were right." The light vanished.

From that night on, Kennette changed. She began to age quickly. But more than that, she softened. She no longer gadded about the neighborhood insulting her neighbors. If they called at her house, she received them kindly and offered them refreshment.

And, on the day before her own death, Marie Thebault astonished the entire parish by attending mass.

The following three stories are from Charles Skinner's collection of tales by Kennette's old French lodger.

Candlelight at Twenty-Fourth Street

In the middle 1700s, an old red mill stood at the foot of what is now 24th Street in Detroit. The keeper of this mill adopted a young Indian girl with the consent of her people, a Pontiac tribe. He raised her as his own daughter, teaching her the ways of the white man.

Among the warriors of the dreaded Pontiac, there was at that time a young brave named Wasson. Wasson watched the maiden as she grew and fell helplessly in love with her. His tribesmen warned him that although she had been born Indian, she was now alien to their tribe, and he should forget her.

But Wasson kept watch over the girl. To his dismay, he soon discovered that she had a secret which she kept from her foster-father. Whenever the miller was away, the girl would put a lighted candle in the window of the mill and a figure wrapped in a military cloak would emerge from the shadows, knock at the door, and be admitted. Wasson finally identified his rival as Colonel Campbell, an English officer, and he was seized by blind rage. He stole into the girl's room through a window and slew her with his hatchet.

After the murder, people began to shun the mill. Those who did venture there often saw the figure of a young Indian maiden with a candle in her hand, walking about in search of her lover. She frightened so many people that finally, in 1795, the mill was torn down to rid it of her ghost. It is claimed by some, however, that to this day the maiden's flickering candle can sometimes be seen along the nearby waterfront.

A Brother's Love

In the early 1800s the Mason family settled on a farm near what is now the city of Detroit. Their two little boys, John and Michael, became friends with Emma Thompson, the daughter of a neighboring farmer. The children went to school and played together throughout their childhood years. Time passed and they grew to be adults. Although Emma loved both the brothers dearly, it was John she chose to marry. Michael bore no grudge. He never married, but the brothers remained fast friends and built homes next to each other. Michael became a frequent and welcome visitor in John and

Emma's home.

One day while the brothers were cutting cord wood, Michael saw that a huge tree was about to fall on John. Screaming, he rushed forward to push his brother out of the way. But it was too late. As the great tree crashed to the ground it pinned both men beneath it. John was not fatally hurt, but his left leg was pinned down by the tree and he could not move it. Michael, however, was mortally wounded, for the trunk of the tree had struck his back above the waist, crushing his torso beneath its weight so that he could not breathe. With his dying breath he told his brother not to worry, for he would get help.

Emma was at home alone, engrossed in her housework, and the children were at school. Suddenly, she heard someone in the kitchen. It was much too early for the men to have returned home. But there was Michael, and she knew immediately that something was terribly wrong. He spoke normally and told her there had been an accident. He assured her John would be all right. Then he instructed her to get help to free her husband and gave her directions to find him. Emma hurried out of the house to enlist the aid of the neighbors, not waiting for her brother-in-law.

Emma and the neighbors reached the fallen tree and freed John quickly. But it was too late to help Michael. He had been dead for more than an hour.

Grand'mere Duchene's Spinning Wheel

Grand'mere Duchene had but one son, Phillippe. He was prosperous and provided a fine home for his wife and family. But he resented having to care for his mother after she was widowed.

Reluctantly, he moved her into a small room in his home, where she lived like a servant rather than a member of the family. Her room was sparsely furnished with a bed, a chair, a small chest, and a spinning wheel. She spent most of her waking hours at this wheel, spinning the thread to be woven into cloth for the family's garments. She did not spin on the Sabbath, however, and being a religious woman she insisted on attending mass every Sunday.

Phillippe himself cared little for the church or its teachings. But public opinion concerned him greatly, so he made his weekly visits to the chapel for show. Grand'mere Duchene was ashamed of her son's attitude and frequently admonished him for his lack of Christian spirit. And so, as his mother lay dying, it was relief rather than grief that prompted Phillippe to make a rash promise to her. He agreed to honor her death by buying 50 masses for the repose of her soul.

Grand'mere Duchene's funeral was a fine one. She was dressed in clothes far finer than any she had worn while living and was laid to rest in a costly casket with great ceremony. But only a short while after she was buried, with an impressive stone marker on her grave, Phillippe promptly forgot her.

One month to the day after Grand'mere Duchene's death, at the very hour of her death, Phillippe looked up from his desk in the study. He had heard what sounded like a spinning wheel. It was certainly strange, for no one had done any spinning in the house since his mother's death. The sound continued and seemed to follow him as he left his study and walked from room to room. As he stopped before the closed door of the room where his mother had spent her final years, the sound became very loud and seemed to be coming from the room itself. He opened the door and stared in horror.

There was Grand'mere Duchene seated at her wheel, spinning.

Phillippe slammed the door, half believing himself to be daft. His mind was surely playing tricks on him. But why? True, he hadn't bought the 50 masses he had promised his mother, but he had certainly given her a fine enough funeral.

The noise of the spinning wheel followed him as he walked through the house. He heard it in his own room. He even heard it when he left the house and walked down the street several blocks.

Day in and day out the sound of the wheel droned on. Phillippe could no longer eat or sleep. At last he knew what he had to do. He sought out the parish priest and bought 50 masses for the repose of his mother's soul. And as he counted out the money, the sound of the spinning wheel became fainter and fainter. It stopped altogether as Phillippe placed the last gold pieces in the hands of the priest.

A Promise Kept

I was greatly honored when Captain Bill Kampfert, a long-time friend of mine, recently renamed his boat "Gundella." A retired naval officer still active in the Reserves, he often teaches classes for new boaters. As owner of W.R.K. Enterprises, he uses the Gundella to run charters on the Detroit River and Lake Erie when he's not busy with his other maritime activities. Bill is a good storyteller and, having spent much of his life on boats, he tells many tales that involve the waterways of this area.

The following story is well known and appears in several old collections of Detroit lore. What makes it special to Bill Kampfert is that early one misty morning in April 1983, he saw the young hunter of this story paddling downstream from Lake St. Clair past the Belle Isle Coast Guard Station with a canoe-load of furs and then he disappeared into the fog. Bill had never seen such a harvest of furs. It occurred to him that it had been at least a century since any trapper had brought furs into Detroit in a canoe. Much later, when he was telling a friend what he had seen, he learned the whole story of Sebastian and Zoe.

Sebastian was a young hunter betrothed to the beautiful Zoe. They planned to marry in the early spring. As winter neared, Sebastian prepared for his long trek to the north where he would spend the winter hunting and collecting the fine furs he would bring back to Detroit by canoe right after the spring thaw. As he kissed his beloved Zoe goodbye, he promised that dead or alive, hell or high water, he would return to her as soon as the ice left the lakes.

The winter seemed unbearably long as Zoe waited for spring and her lover to return. Each day she would go down to the river to see if the ice had broken up. And at last she began to see huge blocks of ice floating down the river from the lakes, and she knew her loneliness would soon come to an end. Day after day she watched for Sebastian's canoe to appear. Then at last there it was, piled high with furs. And there, smiling broadly and waving to her, was her beloved Sebastian. Zoe's heart leapt for joy.

But as the canoe drew nearer, the little craft, its cargo, and her fiance all began to fade before her eyes. Slowly they turned to mist and evaporated into the air. She heard the echo of Sebastian's parting promise, "Dead or alive, I'll come back to you when the ice leaves the lakes."

Year after year, Zoe returned to the river banks and year after year Sebastian kept his promise. Each spring his canoe, laden with furs, drifted down the river as he waved to Zoe on the shore. And each spring, he faded away in the mist.

It is said that to this very day, if you stand on the banks of the Detroit River in the early spring just after the ice leaves the lakes, you can still catch a glimpse — as Bill Kampfert did — of Sebastian keeping his promise to Zoe.

The Curse of L'Anse Creuse

When I was in my early twenties and teaching school in Wayne County, I spent summers working toward my degree and moonlighting at any paying job I could find to help with my tuition. One summer, I was fortunate to get into a program that not only gave me college credit but a small stipend as well. The work involved assisting a professor to conduct a sociological study in Macomb County. My particular assignment took me to St. Clair Shores where I enjoyed myself and found the community to be a pleasant one.

This is a tale that took place on the shores of Lake St. Clair two hundred years ago.

Sometime between 1779 and 1837 when Michigan was young, a man named Lizon came to the village of L'Anse Creuse, northeast of Detroit on the shores of Lake St. Clair. There he opened a taproom that quickly became known as the vilest tavern in the territory.

Fighting, gambling, and carousing were nightly features.

Since he was a newcomer, little was known about Lizon. But it did not take long before it became clear that he was not a pleasant man. He never attended church and was often heard to speak blasphemously of religion in general. Years of perpetual frowning had left two deep vertical lines between his eyes. He had jet black hair that he kept slicked down with oil and dark piercing eyes that never blinked when he glared at someone.

Julienne, the daughter of a local farmer, was a sweet, pious girl, quite shy by nature. Everyone was amazed when Lizon began courting her and even more surprised that Julienne seemed to welcome his attentions. Some people believed that he had used a magic spell to win her favor. Oddly, Lizon joked openly about their relationship, declaring that he had no intention of marrying the girl since he did not believe in religion and thus could certainly not engage in any sort of religious ceremony. Still, Julienne deserted her comfortable home and went to live with Lizon in his disreputable tavern, an unheard-of arrangement for a young woman of her upbringing in those days. Julienne turned a deaf ear to the pleas of her friends and family and refused the counsel of the priest. Indeed, as time passed, Lizon's power seemed to become greater than that of the clergyman; as the tavern gained patrons, the church lost worshippers.

Then one Sunday, Julienne surprised the townsfolk by appearing in church and publicly confessing her wrong-doing. She begged forgiveness. It was the first time she had appeared there or spoken to anyone since her flight from home. She acted as if she had just been roused from a trance. Her father welcomed her home while friends and family rejoiced. All went well until New Year's Eve.

According to a long established custom dating back to the days of the Druids, the young men of the community would don masks and costumes and make the rounds of the settlement, singing and begging food for the poor. That year, when they reached the home of Julienne's father and received his welcome and his goods, their song was interrupted by a cry of distress. Julienne was gone! Lizon, who had been among the masqueraders, had kidnapped her and fled to his tavern. A crowd of villagers pursued them, broke into the tavern and rescued the girl. But it was too late. She had lost her mind and never again regained her sanity. Lizon was captured and taken before the village fathers. In response to their reprimand, he screamed a curse upon the priest, the church, the villagers, and the entire settlement of L'Anse Creuse.

The priest died soon afterward and the morals of the village fell lower and lower. Blight, insects, and bad weather ravaged the fields and orchards.

Whether Lizon was executed or died a natural death has never been agreed upon. But all versions of the tale do agree that as he was being buried in a grave near his tavern, a swarm of fat, filthy snakes crawled up out of the grave, seeming to come from the casket itself. The fog that covered the earth that morning seemed to be blown in from the lake in human forms. The grave rolled like a wave after it had been covered, and when darkness fell, a blue will-o'-the-wisp was seen dancing over it. A violent storm set in that night and the wild, angry winds and water consumed the foundations of the church which fell with a crash into the seething flood. The storm continued through the night until the entire village was washed away.

Over the years, the village was rebuilt. In 1925, 146 years after the first settlers had named it L'Anse Creuse, meaning "deep bay," the village was incorporated and renamed St. Clair Shores.

TWO TALES FROM GROSSE ILE

Except for those who live there or whose work takes them to the businesses and factories of Trenton and Flatrock, or the shopping center of Southgate, very few people seem to visit the downriver area of Greater Detroit. This seems to have suited the beautiful little island community at the mouth of the Detroit River known as Grosse Ile. Accessible by two bridges, the island has managed to maintain much of its early charm and dignity. Except for the construction of a few new subdivisions, it has changed very little since the closing of the old naval base after World War II. It is a residential community that features no great tourist attractions or major shopping malls.

As one drives around Grosse Ile admiring the stately old homes along the waterfront, one house stands out from all the rest because of its elaborate oriental design. Over the years, the house had had many different owners. For a short period in the 1950s it was owned by the Robert McIntyre family.

I was fortunate to be invited to breakfast there one Sunday with a gentleman friend of mine, and Mr. McIntyre treated us to a tour of the building.

Featuring a huge, ornate, golden Chinese dragon in the middle of the living room ceiling, indirect lighting, and sunken marble bathtubs, it was unlike anything I had ever seen. But most exciting to me was the boat well and the underground tunnel leading from behind a concealed panel in the basement to a building across the road and some distance away. The story told to me was that the house had been built during the days of prohibition and the tunnel was part of an elaborate system used by the infamous "Purple Gang" to smuggle liquor into the country from Canada.

Grosse Ile still features an age-old natural sulfur spring and a romantic wishing well. And it has a wealth of wonderful stories about its historic past, ranging from tales of naval battles in the War of 1812 to stories of sentimental love then and later. Here are two of my favorite ghost stories about the island.

Grosse Ile's Will-O'-the-Wisp

The World Book Encyclopedia Dictionary *defines a will-o'-the-wisp as (1) "a moving light appearing at night over marshy places, caused by a combustion of swamp gasses," and (2) "a thing, rarely a person, that deludes or misleads by luring one on." Neither of these definitions really seems to describe Grosse Ile's will-o'-the-wisp.*

Jean L'Esperance and Juliet D'Monet were betrothed. Their bonds had been announced in the church, and the day of their wedding was drawing near when Jean suddenly disappeared. No one knew where he had gone. Some people whispered that perhaps he was not so anxious to marry after all and had run away.

But Juliet knew Jean better than that. She felt certain that he loved her and would always be by her side if he was able. So, saying not a word to anyone, she set out on the third day of his absence to search for him.

All day long she searched in vain, wandering farther and farther into the marshes. At dusk, when she had all but given up hope of ever seeing her sweetheart again, she suddenly stopped in her tracks. Just ahead of her a blue mist had appeared, taking the shape of a human figure. It danced about, beckoning her to follow, and follow she did. As the evening grew darker, the wispy apparition began to glow iridescently as it led her deeper into the swamp.

By now Juliet had lost all sense of direction and was resigned to dying in the swamp. And then, just as she felt she could go no further, she heard Jean's voice calling her name. Guided by the dancing will-o'-the-wisp, she found her beloved engulfed in mire.

With new strength, she found branches to hold out to him, enabling him to free himself. Weakened by hunger and exposure, he leaned on her for support. Juliet led her Jean back to safety, guided by the flickering light that danced on before her.

As they reached the clearing and saw the lights of the cabins, the wispy form vanished.

The Rolling Muff

The husband of a wealthy Detroit matron had long since grown tired of her. He had found a younger companion and yearned to be free of his marriage. But a divorce was unthinkable. Not only would it be difficult to obtain (after all, he was the one at fault), it would also have been very costly. Instead, he worked out an elaborate plan to kill her, hide her body and report her missing. Taking his wife to Grosse Ile, he murdered her there and concealed her body in the marsh.

In the struggle before the murder, the woman had dropped her muff. Realizing this, the man returned later to look for it, for he was afraid someone would find it and begin to wonder how it came to be there. But when he reached for the muff, it took on a life of its own and began to roll about, first eluding him, then chasing him. He became so frightened that he returned to Detroit and confessed his crime.

It was claimed by some that the muff continued to roll about, emitting the putrid odor of death. To see it became an omen of impending trouble.

One story told about the muff concerned two brothers named Tremblay, both of them fishermen. One was a religious man who had made a bargain with St. Patrick, agreeing to share half of the profits from the fish he caught with the good Saint by buying masses for the souls in purgatory. St. Patrick, in return, was to smile upon him and make him prosper. The other brother, while not an evil man, was not as devout. He made fun of this bargain, warning his pious brother to watch out lest he be lured into the water and changed into a trout. For, he teased, hadn't St. Patrick once eaten pork chops on Friday after dunking them in holy water and turning them into fish?

But the pious brother prospered and the other's luck turned from bad to worse. Soon the unlucky brother began to seek solace from the bottle and he was more often drunk than sober.

No one could say for sure whether the poor fellow was drunk when he encountered the rolling muff, for people had only his word for what happened. He declared that he had been cold sober when the dreadful thing chased him off the island. Noticing the odor of his clothing, the pious brother suggested that perhaps he had met a skunk and mistaken it for the phantom muff. But however it happened, from that day forth he drank no more. He joined his brother in his bargain, and St. Patrick had no stauncher allies than the two Tremblays. (The murdered lady may have had a strong dislike for the demon rum.)

Another story often told is that during prohibition, two men bringing ashore a boatload of Canadian liquor encountered the rolling muff. Unable to fight it off, they were running from the muff when they were arrested by federal agents.

The Legend of the Red Dwarf

Perhaps the most frightening of all the phantoms that plagued the early settlers of Detroit was the grotesque little gnome known as the Nain Rouge or the Red Dwarf. Described as a twisted, red-faced creature with a shambling gait, piercing eyes, and decaying teeth that protruded from a slobbering, grinning mouth, the Red Dwarf brought on disaster wherever he appeared.

No one seems to know his origin. When and where this harbinger of doom and destruction came from and why he settled in Detroit are unsolved mysteries. Reported sightings of the Red Dwarf now span a time period of more than 200 years.

Cadillac, the founder of Detroit, was said to have seen the hideous little fellow, striking out at him with a stick. Soon afterward he lost his seigniory and his fortune.

On July 30, 1763, the Red Dwarf was seen running along the banks of the Detroit River. The following day, Captain James Dalyell lost his life and 58 of his officers and men were killed or wounded in the Battle of Bloody Run. A tributary of the Detroit River ran red with their blood.

In the late spring of 1805, the twisted little figure was seen several times hobbling down the city's streets. On June 11 that year, the entire city was destroyed by fire.

General William Hull claimed to have seen the Red Dwarf grinning at him in the fog just before his surrender of Detroit in 1813.

Does the Red Dwarf still exist today?

Some claim to have seen Nain Rouge in the long hot summer of 1967, just before riots shattered the city.

And two Detroit Edison linemen claim to have seen him as recently as March 1, 1976. They say they were sitting in their truck eating their lunches when they spied a strange little creature shinnying up a utility pole. Thinking it was a child, they jumped out of the truck and began yelling at him. He dropped to the ground and scampered away, leering at them over his shoulder. The men could not quite believe their eyes, for neither had ever seen the likes of him before. But on March 2, the city was crippled by the most devastating ice storm in its history, depriving hundreds of thousands of the city's residents of electricity.

III

Out-of-Body Experiences
(Ghosts of the Living)

Sometimes people travel astrally while they are asleep. Here is an example. A few years ago I was teaching a class on occult experiences in Westland, Michigan. One very conscientious student named Elaine Kaiser never missed a class. But one evening I took the roll and she failed to answer. Several others in the class said that they had seen Elaine in the hall just before class. One woman pointed out that she had not looked well. The others agreed and added that although Elaine was usually very well groomed, that night she appeared to be wearing a wrinkled purple pants suit and no makeup at all. Someone reported that even her hair had been uncombed. This was certainly not like Elaine. We assumed she was ill and had returned home.

The next week Elaine appeared in class as well-groomed and perky as ever and apologized for being absent the week before. She explained that both of her children had had the flu and that she had become exhausted from caring for them. She said she had lain down on her couch and fallen asleep, thinking about the class but too tired to attend. When asked what she had been wearing at the time, she replied, "Purple pajamas. Why?"

Astral projection or O.B.E. (out-of-body experience) has been a common occurrence among people throughout recorded history. There have been suggestions that some of the world's major powers have been experimenting with astral projection to spy on their enemies. This may sound like science fiction, but evidence of it appears even in the Bible: in the Second Book of Kings in the Old Testament,

Elisha is believed to have traveled spiritually to the king's bedchamber to learn his battle strategy.

I once attended a party during which the conversation turned to the subject of O.B.E. A medical doctor there told of performing rather routine surgery on a female patient when he happened to look up and there, across the room, was his patient in an upright position, hovering in mid-air watching him. His first thought was that she had died on the table and he was looking at her ghost. But all her vital signs were normal and the body on the table, although anesthetized, was very much alive.

Many people under the influence of anesthesia or sedatives have experienced leaving their bodies and floating about. This can also happen while a person is under the influence of drugs or asleep or even while he or she is wide awake and fully conscious.

Those who have experienced astral projection seem less fearful of death, for they are aware that it is possible to live outside the body in spirit form. They've experienced soul travel and the eventual return to their bodies which then go on functioning normally. When a spirit is disengaged even temporarily from the still very much alive physical body, we refer to it as a living ghost. Like any other ghost, sometimes it can be seen and sometimes not.

The two tales that follow are about ghosts of the living, not the dead. They both took place in the City of Detroit in the 1970s.

The Living Ghost of Rosedale Park

One bright sunny Sunday in early April, George and Emma Lambert went out for a leisurely afternoon drive through a quiet neighborhood in Rosedale Park. Suddenly, Emma gasped and ordered her husband to stop the car. Pointing excitedly at a beautiful old brick home with a "For Sale" sign on the lawn, she exclaimed, "George, that's it! That's the house." Thinking his wife had suddenly taken leave of her senses, George stopped the car. They were certainly not house hunting. In fact, he had thought they were perfectly satisfied with the house they already owned.

When she regained her composure, Emma began to describe a dream she had been having for several months. In it she would be walking through a house unknown to her in daylight but by now very familiar at night. She was certain that the house they were now stopped in front of was the house she had so often visited in her dreams. She was sure that she could describe the inside in detail. Taking a pen and paper from her purse, she began to write down all she could remember about the floor plan, furnishings, and decorating, all the while begging George to go with her and pretend to be prospective buyers of the house.

George wasn't sure. Perhaps it was a plot his wife had concocted to get him to look at a big expensive house they did not need and could not afford. But at last he gave in and they walked up to the door and rang the bell.

A woman opened the door. When she saw the Lamberts, she began screaming and slammed the door in their faces. Emma and George looked at each other in amazement. It certainly was an odd way to treat a prospective buyer inquiring about a house for sale!

But Emma was undaunted. She wasn't going to be put off by a slammed door. She stepped forward and rang the bell again before George (who wanted to turn around and go home) could stop her.

This time the woman opened the door accompanied by her husband. She pointed at Emma and stammered, "Tha . . . that's the woman who's been haunting our house."

Indeed, while Emma slumbered at home in her bed, her dream walks through the house in Rosedale Park had been observed.

There is little doubt that Emma traveled astrally, but no one has been able to explain why she did so or why she chose that particular house to haunt. Perhaps Emma had lived there in another lifetime. The house is old enough for that to be possible, but there is really no evidence to establish it.

Strangely enough, Emma's nightly visits have ceased completely since she visited the house in her waking hours and talked to the people who lived there. The house is no longer haunted but the whole matter remains an unsolved mystery.

Returning Home

Debra Brown loved the house her parents had bought on LaSalle Street in Detroit. It made her feel rich and important just to walk around the large rooms or to sit at the table in the huge formal dining room. Here she had a room of her own that she did not have to share with her sisters. She didn't even mind that because she was the youngest she had been given the smallest of the several bedrooms in the huge old red brick mansion.

Indeed, the whole family was pleased to have found such a lovely home for such a reasonable price after Mr. Brown had been transferred here from Ohio. Having heard stories of what some neighborhoods in Detroit were like, they had dreaded coming here. But this house was magnificent and had helped ease their fears.

After the family had been living in their new home for a month, everyone was awakened one night by Debra's screams. She had always been afraid of the dark, and a small night light had been kept burning in her room. Her parents rushed into her room to see what was wrong, but everything seemed to be in order and no one had passed them in the hall. But Debra, finally quieting down, told them she had seen an old man sitting on the floor in the corner of her room just moments before.

Several times after that Debra told her parents of seeing the same old person in her room or in the hall, and once she claimed she had seen him in the back yard. Her parents were quite certain it was her imagination, and they began to think of taking her to a psychiatrist when something happened to change their minds.

One morning as they started down the stairs together, Mr. and Mrs. Brown saw an elderly man climbing the stairs before them. Mr. Brown was about to ask him who he was and what he wanted, but he faded from view as if he had evaporated. Both had seen the man and were quite certain that they were not losing their sanity. The only explanation seemed to be that the house was haunted. The ghost seemed to wish them no harm, and they soon lost their fear. The family even named the ghost "Charles" and laughed as they discussed him with friends.

After the Browns had been living in the big house for nearly two years, they received a phone call one day from a man who had once lived in the house. He said that years ago his family had moved from the house to Connecticut. He was only 12 years old, but he had never forgotten his childhood home. He said that he still dreamed about it.

The man told them he was visiting relatives in Detroit and would be grateful if the Browns could let him come to see his old home one more time. He was getting on in years and felt certain that this would be his last trip to Michigan. Mr. and Mrs. Brown invited him to come that afternoon. They said they would be glad to show him the improvements they had made to the house.

His arrival turned out to be a shock. They opened the door to find themselves face-to-face with "Charles," and he was indeed very much alive.

Later, in conversation with their guest, the Browns discovered that during the times they had seen "Charles" in their home, the old man had been asleep in his Connecticut home, dreaming about his childhood on LaSalle Street in Detroit and playing with his electric train on the floor in the corner of the room where Debra now slept.

IV

Shades in the Night

Sometimes when the atmospheric conditions are just right, it is possible to see figures, objects, and even whole scenes reflected from the past. They are not ghosts or earthbound spirits. They have no purpose and no message to reveal. They are simply pictures from a time gone by that for some inexplicable reason have reappeared in another era. If they appear more than once, the object or scene never varies. It is like watching a play over and over even though the characters have long since passed away.

One house, with which I am well acquainted, has a long hall on the second floor with four bedrooms and a bath opening onto it. Visitors often compliment the host and hostess on the fine antique chest in that hallway. But, my friends, there is no such chest in that house, and there never has been as long as the present owners have lived there. But long ago, some former resident most likely had such a piece of furniture that graced that hallway. And for some unexplained reason, its shade can still be seen there.

The Kitchen

In the upstairs bedroom of her small frame house in Plymouth, Michigan, Margie awoke from a sound sleep. The illuminated dial of the alarm clock showed exactly 4:00 a.m. She lay there wondering what had awakened her. Her husband was alseep at her side and other than his deep, regular breathing, there was no sound. Margie could not go back to sleep.

Quietly, not waking her husband, she got out of bed and walked across the room to the window. It was a cold winter's night. Big, fluffy snowflakes filled the air. It had been snowing for quite some time for the ground was completely covered and there was not a track of any kind in sight. Margie went downstairs to the kitchen to fix herself a cup of hot tea. She walked into the kitchen and turned on the light.

But it was not her kitchen.

The room had been completely changed somehow. It seemed as if she had stepped into a kitchen from the 1930s. There was a hand pump in a chipped enamel sink and a pail and dipper under the spout. A big black woodburning cook stove took up one whole side of the room. On the floor lay a flowered linoleum rug, with bare wooden boards visible around the edges. A patterned oil cloth covered a round wooden table in the center of the room. And seated around it were three people Margie had never seen before. They seemed deep in conversation. Their lips moved and yet there was no sound. No one seemed to notice that she was there. Margie suddenly felt as if she were an intruder in someone else's home.

Totally mystified, she rushed back upstairs, woke her husband, and begged him to come downstairs with her. But when they reached the kitchen, nothing was amiss. The gleaming electric range, the automatic dishwasher, the frost-free refrigerator, and the stainless steel double sink were all in their proper places. The floor was covered wall-to-wall with its rust-colored carpeting. And there were no people in the room.

Margie still insists she was fully awake and did not dream she was in another kitchen as her husband suggests. But nothing like this had ever happened to her before and has never happened again.

A Victorian Shade

On the lower east side of Detroit, not far from the Belle Isle Bridge, stands a neighborhood of beautiful historic homes known as Indian Village. One of these houses, a fine old Victorian mansion from the 1890s, is haunted. Not by a ghost, but by a shade.

An attractive woman about 40 years old with thick brown hair pulled severely back and twisted into a knot at the back of her neck suddenly appears at the top of the stairway. She is wearing a tight-waisted long grey dress with a white collar and white cuffs. She is crying mournfully into a blue lace handkerchief. Slowly she descends the stairs and stops for a moment at the bottom step to wipe her eyes. Then she abruptly turns to the right and walks down the hall to the butler's pantry where she disappears.

Over the past 27 years (and perhaps much longer), everyone who has lived in that house on Seminole Street has seen her as have many of the guests who have visited the house. Who she is, why she is crying, and what became of her, no one knows. She never talks.

Attempts to communicate with her through seances always fail, for she is not really a ghost. She is a shade acting out a scene from the past, a scene destined to be played out for all eternity.

No Vacancy

Before being transferred to Detroit where he now lives, Richard made several business trips to the city for his company in Atlanta, Georgia. It was on one of these trips that he had the most unusual experience of his life.

Richard arrived at the Detroit Metropolitan Airport at 11 a.m., with just enough time to eat lunch and meet his client at 1 p.m. The meeting was very successful, and he returned to the airport late that afternoon to catch his 6 p.m. flight home. When he went to the airline desk to check in, he was told that there had been a mix-up in the reservations and his flight was overbooked; there was no seat for him. The ticket agent tried in vain to book him on other airlines, but they too were completely sold out and there was nothing available to Atlanta until the next morning. Richard was not upset; he would just get a room in a hotel and after a good night's sleep, go home refreshed in the morning.

It wasn't so easy. There were several large conventions in town, and all the nearby hotels were filled to capacity. After making many unproductive phone calls to hotels farther from the airport, Richard finally gave up and hailed a cab, asking the driver's help in finding a room for the night. But there were "no vacancy" signs at all the motels they passed. Then, the driver turned to Richard and startled him with an odd question. "How do you feel about ghosts?" he asked.

"Ghosts?" echoed Richard, wondering what the man was getting at.

"Ghosts!" answered the cabbie. "Do you or don't you believe in them?"

"Of course not," said Richard with disdain. "There are no such things."

"Well then," said the driver, "you wouldn't mind sleeping in a haunted room, would you?" Richard chuckled.

The driver explained that his friend worked as the night manager of a small motel in Inkster where there was one room that was always empty. They no longer offered it to customers even when all the others were filled. It seems that once upon a time, a married man who was cheating on his wife had rented the room as a place to entertain his girlfriend. His wife had followed them there, broken into the room, and shot them to death before turning herself in to police. The room wasn't rented out because everyone who had slept there after the murders claimed that it was haunted. The cabbie was certain he could persuade his friend to rent it for the night to a man who didn't believe in ghosts.

By now, it was nearly 10 p.m. Richard was exhausted and told the driver to take him to the "haunted room." The cabbie drove to a small motel on Michigan Avenue. Although a far cry from the Hilton, Richard found it to be clean and in good repair. He thanked the cab driver and tipped him generously.

After taking a hot shower, Richard went straight to bed and slept well until he awoke with an uneasy feeling at 3:33 a.m. (Telling the story later, he was very sure of the time since he remembered thinking how strange it was to see three 3's in a row on his digital watch. Lying in bed, he felt certain he was not alone. Then he heard someone moving about. As his eyes became accustomed to the faint light coming in around the draperies, he saw them.

Just inside the door, locked in a passionate embrace, stood a man and a woman. Richard coughed, hoping they would realize they were in the wrong room. But the couple continued their love play, oblivious to his presence. He heard the woman giggle and the man chuckle softly and then watched as their shadowy figures moved across the room to the foot of his bed. He knew he needed to stop them before they began to undress. He coughed again, louder this time. Again they ignored him. Now, still not wanting to embarrass them, but feeling that he had to make his presence known, Richard reached out and turned on the light at his bedside. To his astonishment, he found that he was completely alone in the room. The door was locked and the chain bolt was in place just as he had left it. He searched the bathroom and the closet and found both empty. He had been certain beyond doubt only a few moments before that there had been two other people in the room. Now they were gone. But Richard decided not to wait for an explanation. He dressed as quickly as he could and left the motel. At an outdoor phone, he called a cab and was relieved to see that the driver who arrived was not the same cabbie who had found him the room. He didn't want to have to say that he'd changed his mind about ghosts.

Richard returned to the airport where he spent the rest of the night in the well-lighted waiting room.

V

Poltergeists

Most dictionaries define a poltergeist as a noisy or mischievous ghost. This is not exactly accurate. A ghost is an entity, a separate and distinct being. When a ghost haunts, it is usually with a purpose and usually because it wants to communicate with the living. A poltergeist, on the other hand, is not a separate entity with a purpose of its own. And although it may cause a lot of noise and action, it does not really communicate. It is, in effect, the result of human energy. Let me explain.

All humans, whether or not they realize it, possess a certain amount of kinetic power that can be used to move objects without touching them. This is sometimes referred to as psychokinesis or teleportation. With practice, many people can develop and control this power, enabling them to make a hanging object (such as a mobile, a pendulum lamp, or a hanging plant) sway or move in a circular pattern without touching it. Groups of people working together — as in a seance, for example — can produce energies that unite and seem to take on a personality of their own. A witches' cone of power is an excellent example. But you need not be a witch to have this power. A simple seance often produces it, without the presence or involvement of spirits.

A group of people sits around a table with everyone's hands on top so that each person's little finger touches his or her neighbor's and their hands form an unbroken chain. Lights are dimmed to make it easier for the participants to concentrate. If all the members of the group do concentrate, it is possible for them to work up energy that is so electric that it can be felt by others in the room outside the circle. Often, tables rock, rap, tip, and even seem to jump about the room of their own accord. I have seen seances in which the participants had to stand up, leave their chairs, and follow the table to avoid breaking the circle. Once movement starts, light can be turned up, people can laugh and talk, and nothing short of breaking the circle seems to stop the action.

Such action is the product of human energies, not spirits. Although not consciously, the members of a circle are providing the energy that moves the table.

A poltergeist is an unpremeditated release of energy of this sort. It can be produced by just one person or a combination of energies from more than one. The people causing this energy release are unaware that they are responsible and usually believe they are being visited by a ghost.

Interestingly, poltergeist activity often occurs in households with teenagers. This is not difficult to understand. Teenagers are more likely to be frustrated and anxious than nearly any other age group, due in part to the biological changes taking place in their bodies and to the way we as adults are treating them. First we tell them they are no longer children and that they should and act grown up. Then, when they try to emulate adult behavior, we tell them they are not old enough and they are still children. If a teen openly reacts and vents his anger by talking back, slamming doors, and so on, there is little likelihood of trouble with a poltergeist. It is when the young person represses anger that his or her pent-up frustrations can cause the kinetic energy that gives rise to havoc. Then everyone becomes frightened and believes there is a ghost in the house.

The following story, covered by the Detroit News, *the* Detroit Free Press, *the* National Enquirer, *and the* Mellus Newspapers *from 1970-1972, is an excellent example of this phenomenon.*

The Lincoln Park Poltergeist

The McMasters family lived a quiet life in a quiet neighborhood in the Detroit suburb of Lincoln Park. Doris McMasters was the dominating member of the family. Crippled by a leg problem, she did little to help herself, depending totally on her husband and son who catered to her every wish.

Walter, her husband, was an extremely handsome man but one

with no spark of enthusiasm about anything. It was as if he had long since lost all hope for any excitement in life. His daily routine consisted of getting up, going to work at the Ford factory, coming back home in the evening and sitting with the rest of the family, usually watching television until it was time for bed.

He had once enjoyed bowling, but when his wife could no longer go out, it seemed unfair for him to do so. So he had quit bowling.

Their son, Larry, had quit school at age 16 to stay home and take care of his mother. Larry was a big boy, very docile, and quite friendly. But his lifestyle was certainly not that of an average young man. At the age of 19, when his family's story finally became known, he had never driven a car or had a date. He had no friends his own age, and his only outings were weekly shopping trips with his father to the supermarket. His daily activities consisted mainly of cleaning, cooking, keeping house, waiting on his mother, and watching television. His only hobby was stamp collecting.

One winter evening, while the family was sitting in the living room, they heard a sharp crack and found that a cue stick lying on the pool table in the adjacent recreation room had broken in two. It was winter, they reasoned, and perhaps the dry heat and lack of humidity had caused this freak accident. But the following night, there was another incident. Again, they were sitting quietly, Larry reading a book while his father and mother played cards. Suddenly, magazines that had been stacked neatly on the coffee table flew up and scattered about the room. No door or window had been opened and no draft had entered the room. Certainly, no human hand had caused them to fly about.

The McMasters became understandably upset. They believed their house to be haunted, and what was to follow certainly strengthened this feeling. In the next several weeks doors would open and close by themselves, the toilet would flush when no one was in the bathroom, and inanimate objects took on lives of their own, moving about from place to place. The McMasters mentioned these things to no one, and quickly and quietly put their house up for sale. It was soon sold, and the family moved into another house just a few blocks away.

But the McMasters soon realized that they had not out-run their problem. In their new home, just as in the one they had left, lights flickered off and on, rocking chairs rocked with no one in them, and weird thumps and bumps could be heard at all hours of the day and night.

Around this time, both major Detroit newspapers featured columns designed to help readers solve problems of all sorts. The column in the *Detroit News*, called "Contact Ten," was handled by a panel of ten writers and advisors. The *Detroit Free Press* column was "Action Line." Readers could call or write either of these to seek help with unusual situations.

The McMasters first called Action Line. The *Free Press* called me, asking me to accompany the reporter covering the case when she visited the McMasters in their home. After talking at length with all three members of the family, I came to the conclusion that what was troubling them was not a ghost but a poltergeist and carefully explained to them the difference. They refused to believe this and begged me to perform an exorcism. When I said that I felt it would be a waste of time since there was no ghost to begin with, they implored me to do it anyway.

I discussed the matter with two psychologists from Wayne State University. Both felt that if such a ritual were enacted and the McMasters believed in it, it might possibly serve to lay their "ghost" to rest. I had my doubts, but since it would do no harm, I decided to go through with it.

At the appointed time, I arrived at the house in Lincoln Park. Mr. and Mrs. McMasters, their son Larry, and the *Free Press* reporter were all assembled in the living room to observe the ceremony. I began to bless the house with earth, air, fire, and water, according to tradition. Halfway through the procedure there was sudden pandemonium. Doors began slamming all through the house; clattering, clanging, and rattling came from all directions; whirring and buzzing sounds filled the air and grew louder and louder. Mrs. McMasters began screaming. Her husband tried to comfort her and Larry threw up. The *Free Press* reporter rushed out of the house. To her credit she returned a few minutes later, saying she had gone outdoors to see what might be going on out there to account for the noise.

When the ritual was completed and things had quieted down, the McMasters seemed to be very pleased. They were certain that everything was now all right and the house had been rid of its "evil spirits."

I still had my doubts, and time proved me correct.

Nothing unusual occurred during the next two months. But ten weeks after the "exorcism," thumpings, bumpings, and weird happenings once again began to plague the McMasters family. This time they called Contact Ten.

The *Detroit News* called in experts from Duke University in North Carolina. After investigating the phenomenon they, too, felt that it was not a ghost but a poltergeist causing all the commotion, and that it was the result of the frustrations and anxieties of the people who lived in the house. They suggested that if Larry were allowed to go back to school, join the service, or in some other way get back into the mainstream of life with others his own age, the whole matter might well be solved.

Mr. and Mrs. McMasters refused to accept this view and would not permit Larry to leave home since they felt he was needed to care for his mother. When therapy for Mrs. McMasters was suggested — so that she could learn to do more for herself in spite of her handicap — that idea was also scorned.

When last heard of, the McMasters family was still living as they had been before their troubles began and still believed they were being "haunted."

The Ghosts of Bower's Harbor Inn

Since so many people have had unusual experiences in the house in this story, it seems clear that some sort of psychic phenomenon is occurring there. But I believe it is probably a combination of shades and poltergeists that account for these events rather than a ghost.

Jutting out into Traverse Bay at Traverse City is a finger of land known as Old Mission Peninsula. Almost 18 miles long and a mile and a half wide, it is unusually beautiful. Driving or hiking around the peninsula, one comes upon a link with the past: two old cemeteries, one on either side of Center Road, protect graves dating back to the early 1900s. Along the peninsula's nature trails and sandy beaches, it isn't hard to imagine a time when the wooded area was inhabited only by Indians. Nor is it difficult to feel the awe that must have overpowered the early European explorers and settlers who first saw how beautiful the area was.

It is no wonder that J.W. Stickney, who arrived on Old Mission Peninsula from Chicago in the late 1800s with his wife, Genevive, chose the spot to be their home.

While J.W. was building his fortune in lumber and steel, Genevive was busy as well. Behind the farmhouse where they lived was a smaller building known locally as Mrs. Stickney's jam kitchen. It was there that she, assisted by her servants, prepared her jams, jellies, preserves, fruit brandies, and liqueurs. It was said she was also adept at wine-making. Her products were so good that her husband and a relative took the advice of friends and made a business of marketing them. The tasty brandies were so unique that the Stickneys feared they would be stolen and kept them under lock and key in an underground fruit cellar on the property.

As time went by, the Stickneys prospered and before long they replaced their farmhouse with a home befitting a lumber baron in that grand era. It was a mansion that still stands today on Mission Peninsula, surrounded by majestic oaks and stately pines overlooking Grand Traverse Bay.

Furnishing their new home, Genevive had a special gilt-edged mirror custom-made. She was a plump woman, and the mirror was designed in a special way to make her appear thinner. Approaching the looking glass, her reflection lost pounds with every step. Another of the Stickney's treasures was an elevator J.W. had installed as he grew older.

The historic old building changed hands several times after the Stickneys passed away. In 1959 Jim and Fern Bryant bought it and converted it into a commercial dining establishment still known today as Bower's Harbor Inn. They sold it in 1964 to Toni Scharling and her close friends, Bruce and Sally Towner. Toni Scharling and the Towners believe that the Bryants were completely honest when they said they felt the house was haunted. The Bryants said there had been weird happenings such as lights turning on and off, glass breaking, and objects falling when no one was near. The new owners took these tales with a grain of salt. They had loved the building on sight and planned to use it as both a commercial establishment and as a residence for their combined families. But before long, they had a few weird tales of their own to tell.

One day, a patron of the restaurant came rushing out of the room where Genevive's unusual mirror was standing. Almost colliding with Toni Scharling, she was trembling with fright. She said she had been alone in the room playfully enjoying looking at herself in the mirror, when suddenly she saw the reflection of another woman standing behind her gazing over her shoulder into the looking glass.

The woman was dressed in clothing from another era, her long hair pulled back into an upswept twist held in place by an ornate comb. When the guest turned to speak to her, there was no one there.

Since then others have reported catching glimpses of the spectral lady when looking in the mirror.

During the time the Scharlings and the Towners lived upstairs over the restaurant, objects were often tossed at them by an unseen pitcher. They might have blamed the children, but these incidents occurred when the children were not present. Objects would disappear and later reappear as if never moved. There was unexplained knocking in the walls and rapping on doors or inside closets. One night the French doors connecting a porch on the north end of the building to the dormitory-style room where the eight girls slept suddenly flew open with a loud "whoosh." The doors, difficult to open even when not locked, had been firmly secured for the night. There had been no wind and had there been, it alone could not have opened the doors.

Another baffling incident occurred in the restaurant one evening during the dinner hour. Several diners had already been seated, none of them anywhere near the salad bar. Without warning, a dish of food from the center of the salad bar to hurl itself through the air and crash to the floor. It was as if someone had picked it up and thrown it.

These eerie activities continued long after Toni and her friends sold the restaurant.

Ernest Hall denied believing in ghosts, but he could offer no other explanation for some of the things that took place there in the late 1970s when he was acting manager. In the 1970s during the winter months, the restaurant was open only on weekends for the dinner hour. Late one night, Ernest was busy in his office with paperwork until after 1 a.m. As he was leaving for the night, he noticed that the basement lights were on. He turned them off and locked up the building. When he returned at eight the next morning, he found the lights on again. Again, he turned them off and locked up before going out to take care of business at the bank and post office. Returning to the restaurant after his errands, he found the lights on once again. The owner and the cook were the only other two people with keys. Ernest, not a believer in ghosts, called both of them. Neither had been in the building since the day before. The electricians he then consulted said that, yes, faulty wiring could account for the lights going on, but they pointed out that this was not the case here. The light switch had been found in the "on" position and could be turned off each time.

And there was another mystery. The door leading into the upstairs ladies' room always caught on the carpeting, making it difficult to open and close. Yet, at night, after the restaurant was closed and Ernest Hall was alone in the building, the door would suddenly slam shut with a bang, although no one had been anywhere near it.

Since 1974, the Bower's Harbor Inn has been owned and operated by Schelde Enterprises and has received national recognition for its excellent cuisine. Behind the main building, in what was once the servants' quarters, is a less formal dining place called the Bowery. It offers antique country charm with cottage-style windows overlooking hills and cherry orchards. Mission Peninsula still has the highest concentration of cherry trees anywhere in the world.

But odd things are still taking place in the old inn. The old elevator, for instance. Even before the present owners closed it down, people had been hesitant to board J. W. Stickney's old elevator. It had been rumored that one customer had once come face-to-face with J.W. himself as he traveled up and down between the floors. The elevator has been out of operation now for years. But not long ago, it started up all by itself and moved slowly from one floor to another.

Another day, Randy Sharp, the restaurant's senior manager, was alone in the building. He wanted to put away some things in the second storeroom. To reach this room one must pass through another storeroom first. One door leads into the first room and, at the back of that room, another door leads into the second room. Randy passed through the first room and into the second. Although there were no outside doors or windows open to account for even the faintest draft, both doors closed behind him.

Odd things are indeed still occurring at Bower's Harbor Inn.

VI

Haunted Graveyards

Most ghosts seem to have a reason for haunting. More often than not, they seem to want to convey a message to the living. Therefore, it would be rather unlikely that they would hang around cemeteries lurking behind tombstones where living humans seldom visit. Still, some have been seen around graveyards. These ghosts, rather than trying to communicate with the living, appear to be seeking out spirits of others like themselves. But why do they cling to their earthly appearances and not go on to other planes?

The Crouch Murders

My friend Gloria Ladd is a respected author and illustrator who has studied and taken part in psychic experiments conducted in the US, the former USSR, and China. She was hard at work gathering material for a new book, "The Crouch Murders," when she invited me to accompany her to the gravesites of some of the victims of the Crouch mass murder. After hearing a synopsis of the Crouch story, I became fascinated and readily accepted her invitation.

On November 21, 1883, in the then-small community of Jackson, Michigan, there was a hideous mass murder. It is still unsolved to this day. All of those even remotely involved have long since died and taken their secrets with them to the grave.

Jacob Crouch, 74, his daughter, Eunice White, 32 and in her ninth month of pregnancy, Henry White, 30, Eunice's husband, and a 24-year-old man named Moses Polley, who was visiting the Crouch family from out of town, were all shot to death while sleeping in their beds. This crime was carried out during a treacherous thunderstorm that toppled many trees and caused untold damage to outbuildings, not only on the Crouch property but on neighboring farms for miles around. Two months later on January 2, 1884, the naked body of Susan Halcomb, Jacob Crouch's remaining daughter, was found on the floor of her bedroom. It appeared that she had died writhing in pain from poison administered by an unknown hand. James Fay, who worked as a farm hand for Jacob Crouch, and later for his son-in-law Daniel Halcomb, Susan's husband, was also found dead shortly thereafter. Some say his death was a suicide; others claim it too was a murder.

In the years that followed, several men were brought to trial for these six crimes (seven, if you count the unborn child whose mother was gruesomely murdered). But none of them was ever convicted. Jacob Crouch was buried in a tiny cemetery at the corner of Horton and Reynolds Roads, a mile from the Crouch home. Eunice and her husband lie five miles away in the large St. John's Cemetery within the Jackson city limits. No two burial sites could differ more. Jacob's grave is neglected and overgrown in an area that looks much as it did a hundred years ago. Eunice's grave is near a well-traveled highway in a cemetery still in use today. New graves lie beside old ones and the grounds around them are neatly trimmed.

Tradition has it that Eunice rises from her grave each year on the anniversary of the murders and travels to her father's tomb, and that the old man's ghost appears to greet her.

The first visit Gloria Ladd and I made to the graves was on a bright summer afternoon in June 1989. First we inspected the St. John's gravesite and then we drove out into the country to see Jacob's final resting place. The reunions between father and daughter are said to take place at the old Reynolds Cemetery, never at St. John's. After visiting both sites it is not hard to understand why. Upon entering the Reynolds Cemetery, one experiences an eerie quiet. My first impulse was to lower my voice to a whisper. I would not have been surprised if an apparition had materialized at any moment. None did. Gloria and I promised each other that we would return on November 21 and see if we might be lucky enough to witness Eunice's reunion with her father.

In the past, the specters had been reported to appear any time from dusk on the 21st to dawn the 22nd. Not wanting to miss anything that November, we arrived well before dark at the Reynolds graveyard and parked our car at an angle that afforded us both a wide view of the little cemetery. We were warmly dressed and fortified with blankets and a thermos jug of hot coffee.

The evening passed uneventfully. By eleven o'clock, we were becoming stiff from sitting so long and got out of the car to stretch. And, after drinking so much coffee we both needed to relieve ourselves. With the aid of a flashlight, we picked our way toward an old out-house behind an abandoned building on the opposite side of the cemetery. Around the graves we went, making our way through the tangled underbrush. On the way back to the car we began to realize that neither of us was as young as she used to be. It was a very cold night and two arthritic old women would certainly have been better off at home by the fire than out in the middle of an unlit cemetery, ghost hunting.

Then we stopped dead. It was a clear night, but at the west end of the graveyard we saw a patch of fog resembling a small cloud. Our aches and pains were completely forgotten. Mesmerized, we watched as the mass of vapor drifted gently across the cemetery. There was little or no wind, but the cloud moved smoothly and evenly, crossing directly in front of us. When it reached Jacob's grave it stopped and hung in the air for several seconds before fading completely away.

We went back to the car and watched diligently for the rest of the night. Nothing more happened.

What was it that we saw? A ghost? And if so, was it Eunice visiting her father or Jacob returning to his own grave after visiting his daughter? The fog cloud had not taken the shape of a man or woman, nor any other real shape at all. Was the visit completed or did we scare it away? Had it faded because it became aware of our presence?

Should you decide to visit the haunted grave site on the anniversary of the grisly Crouch murders, take a word of advice from one who has been there. Dress warmly or your shivers may come from the weather and not from looking at ghostly forms. And take along a flashlight, not to shine on the specters, but to see where you are stepping. There are no street lights on those country roads and it can be very, very dark even on a moonlit night in Reynolds graveyard.

The Spirits of Butler Cemetery

Close to Detroit, in the city of Westland, the Butler Cemetery on Henry Ruff Road is said to be the site of frequent hauntings. Whether these are the work of ghosts, human hoodlums, active imaginations, or a combination of the three, I leave to you to decide.

The principal of nearby Woodson School told me that over the years several of his students have reported seeing ghostly figures haunting the place. But, he is quick to point out, children do tend to have active imaginations. When I asked if he himself had ever seen a ghost there, he answered, "Who, me? No way are you going to get me close enough to that place to see anything!!"

But Tony Pointer is not a child. He is a grown man with children of his own, a sober man whose sanity has never been questioned. Tony claims to have seen ghosts at Butler Cemetery not once but twice. The first time, late at night, he saw the figure of a woman dressed in white crossing the road in front of the cemetery. He swerved to avoid hitting her, and she vanished in front of his eyes. A year later, he was again passing the cemetery. This time, it was just at dusk on a foggy evening in late October. The lady in white was standing in the graveyard next to a large monument. Nearby stood a second figure, a man dressed in what looked like a grey uniform. Tony stopped his car to get a better look at them, and they both seemed to dissolve into the fog. There were no other parked cars in sight. He was certain that the figures he had seen were not just ordinary people visiting the grave of a loved one, as has been suggested.

"No sir," asserts Tony, "those were ghosts. I saw them, and nobody is going to convince me otherwise!"

It was 1980 when I first heard of this haunted site, and I decided to visit the place myself.

Even at high noon with the sun brightly shining, my companion and I both felt an eerie sensation when we rounded the curve at that neglected graveyard. The place was overgrown with grass and weeds and strewn with broken branches. Wild grapevines clung to what remained of a wire fence surrounding it, and a rusty gate hung on broken hinges. The property across the road and on both sides of the cemetery was vacant. An old abandoned mansion was the closest building. It must have been very beautiful once, but now it stood empty, its windows gone and its doors hanging open. A little unoccupied house, just to the south of the larger one, was boarded up and surrounded by discarded furniture.

We parked our car at the gate and entered the cemetery on foot. I have always enjoyed exploring old burial grounds. I was soon occupied with reading the old grave markers, trying to imagine the long ago lives of those whose earthly remains lay beneath the tombstones.

Suddenly, I was yanked out of my day dreaming by the voice of my companion urging me to come quickly and see what she had discovered. I climbed to the top of the hill where she was standing and was stunned by what I saw.

An old grave appeared to have been recently dug up and hastily refilled. What looked like a blonde wig lay on the ground nearby. I stooped to pick it up but quickly dropped it again when I saw it was not a wig at all but the dried scalp of a woman long dead. Closer examination of the grave revealed a shoulder bone sticking out of the dirt piled over the grave. To one side of the grave lay some neatly stacked boards from a rotted wooden casket, some with bits of a faded silk lining still clinging to them. Using a twig from a fallen branch, I again picked up the scalp and carried it gingerly back to the car where we put it in a paper bag. Then we drove quickly to the Westland Police Station and turned the bag and its contents over to an officer who took our report.

Several days later, I called the police to learn what more they had discovered. I was told that nothing was amiss. The grave, they said, had been dug up by animals. I was puzzled and replied that this seemed highly unlikely since shovel marks had been clearly visible and the casket boards had been neatly stacked in a pile. The officer at the other end of the phone explained this away, saying that most likely someone else had happened along before us and tried to straighten up the damage.

I still personally believe that the "animals" who disturbed the grave were two-legged ones either hoping to steal jewelry from a long buried corpse or planning some other such foul play. But since the police were not interested, I let the matter drop.

I should also mention, though, that over the years, there have been several automobile accidents on the short stretch of road at Butler Cemetery. A few months after I was there, I read in the paper that another young man had died there when his car crashed into the hill. The road curves abruptly at the hill and that alone could account for the high accident rate. But there are those like Tony Pointer who believe that anyone could lose control of a vehicle in the presence of a ghost.

VII

Helpful Haunts

Strange as it may seem, some ghosts seem to haunt for the sole purpose of helping the living — perhaps someone they have known, a loved one, or a complete stranger. The Grosse Ile Will-o'-the'-Wisp (Chapter II) was this sort. Many of these ghosts have actually been known to save lives, such as Michael did in "A Brother's Love," (Chapter II), while others simply seem to want to make this world a little less lonely. Here are a few more recent tales about helpful ghosts.

The Lady in the Church Yard

The night was dark and foggy. Norman was on his way to pick up his wife who had been attending a baby shower in the basement of the new church in Farmington. He drove into the parking lot and decided not to stop there, but to circle behind the church and bring the car up to the doors at the front of the building where his wife would see him.

As he neared the back of the lot and began to turn toward the rear of the building, he saw standing directly in front of him the figure of a woman who looked exactly like his mother. He slammed on his brakes and brought the car to a screeching halt. He knew it could not be his mother for she had been dead nearly two years. The woman remained standing in front of the car, gazing directly at him. And now he felt he was losing his senses, for indeed it could have been no one but his beloved mother.

Norman opened the car door and stepped out into the mist. He

approached the front of the car where he had seen his mother standing. No one was there. But what he saw made him gasp in horror.
What he had thought were bushes in the fog were really tree tops.
The church had been built on a ledge overlooking a ravine. There
was no driveway behind the building. Had he driven just a few feet
further, his car would have plunged over the ledge and into the
ravine below.

Lost in the Woods

The city of Oscoda, Michigan, lies just north of Saginaw Bay on the
shores of Lake Huron. Although this bustling community is as
up-to-date as any in the state, it has deep ties with the past. Ghosts
still rise up from the ashes of Au Sable, Iosco County's oldest settlement, a small community that was consumed in a terrible forest fire
in 1911. To this very day, it remains the monthly meeting place of an
age-old coven of witches whose members still dance naked on the
banks of the river. Not far away lies Lake Solitude. Historians tell us
that it was once part of Lake Huron; today the two are connected
only by a small creek, no more than a few yards wide at some points,
which flows into Tawas Bay. In the past, it was called Mud Lake and
then Cranberry Lake. Several generations of native Iosco County
residents have grown up on legends of a large boat that lies buried in
the sand and silt of Lake Solitude. Old timers believe that it is the
wreck of the Griffin (the legendary ship of the French explorer
LaSalle) and that the ghosts of its crew still haunt the shores.

But Mike and his two friends, all from Redford Township, were
not looking for ghosts when they rented a small cabin in the woods
just outside of Oscoda. It was November, 1979, and hunting season
had just opened. The three men and hundreds like them had invad-
ed the North in search of deer. One of the trio had bagged a six-point
buck on the first day. Two days later, the second man got his deer.
Both men continued to go out into the woods with Mike each day
hoping to help him bring down a deer so he would not have to go
home empty handed. But luck was not with them, and soon their
week's vacation was over. It was time to return home, and Mike had
not even seen a deer.

The day of the return trip, Mike arose very early telling his
friends he was going to give it one more try. They said they would
stay behind to load the van for the trip back home. Mike promised to

be back by noon so they could get an early start and be back in Detroit before dark.

It was a cool crisp day. There had been a light dusting of snow the night before. Not far into the woods, Mike discovered fresh deer tracks and excitedly began to follow them. But as the morning wore on, the sun melted the snow and he lost the trail. Finally resigned to going home without a deer, he started back, planning to take the road. It was nowhere in sight, and he quickly realized that he was lost.

By his watch, it was already 1 p.m., and Mike had promised to be back at the cabin by noon. He began shouting, hoping that by this time his friends were out looking for him. After another hour of futile walking and calling out every few minutes with no response, he became frightened. He was exhausted and very hungry. He sat down under a tree to think. The forest was unnaturally quiet. There were no sounds, not even a bird chirping in the distance. Utterly dejected, Mike did something he had seldom done. He began to pray.

As he did, there was suddenly a crackling in the bushes. He looked up to see a young woman standing before him. Dressed in a long coat, knitted cap, and mittens, the woman smiled at Mike and asked him what he was doing down on the ground. When he explained, she assured him that she would lead him to safety. Her father owned a farm not far from there, she said, and she was well-acquainted with the woods. Before long they were in sight of the road. Now knowing his way back to the cabin, Mike thanked the woman profusely. She smiled at him again.

And then she began to disappear.

First, the woman's image seemed blurred and soon he could see right through her. Then she was gone completely.

Mike rushed along the road and back to the safety of the cabin. His friends had just returned from searching for him. They said they weren't sure whether to rejoice because he was back and safe or be angry for the trouble he had caused them. By this time, all three were very tired and it was too late to be back home before dark, so they decided to stay one more night and leave early the next morning. Since all of their gear had already been packed, they agreed to go into the nearby town and have supper in a restaurant. There they could call home to their wives and explain the delay.

After their meal, they stopped in a local bar for beer. Feeling quite comfortable now, Mike told about the girl who had saved his life and how she had vanished before his eyes. His friends stared at him in disbelief. He hadn't had enough beer yet to be intoxicated, and they began to wonder if Mike's mind had been affected by his ordeal in the forest. But the bartender, who had been listening to the story, wasn't at all surprised.

"That was Leona," he said. "Her family used to have a farm back in there, though they're all gone now." He said Leona had been shot nearly 50 years before by a hunter who mistook her for a deer. Since then, her ghost had helped several people find their way out of the woods.

Grandma Sophie

Pete and Nancy had five fine children, all very young. The family lived in a neat frame house on Appleton Street in Detroit. Pete's father lived in a nearby nursing home, but Pete and Nancy would bring him home for dinner almost every evening. They were a close-knit group with strong family loyalties.

Pete's mother had died before he and Nancy were married. She had never met Nancy or any of the children. Nonetheless, she seemed to demonstrate her love for each of them in many ways. Nancy and Pete had felt her presence on several critical occasions.

One day while Nancy was busy in the kitchen, she heard the phone ring in the living room, although the extension phone in the kitchen did not ring at the same time. Thinking that the ringer on the kitchen extension might be broken, she picked it up anyway, but heard only a dial tone. Seconds later the living room phone rang again. This time she went into the living room to answer it, and again, there was no one on the line. But as she turned back toward the kitchen, she discovered her three-year-old sitting on the couch with a bottle of pills she had taken from her mother's purse. Nancy believed that the ring of the phone may have saved her child's life.

Another day, Nancy had put the baby to sleep in an upstairs bedroom. The room had a window that opened onto a lower part of the roof. It was summertime and, although the window was open, the screen was firmly in place. As soon as the child was asleep, Nancy went downstairs to do the laundry.

A short while later Nancy heard someone calling her name. She went to the door, but no one was there. She was about to return to her laundry when she heard her name again, called by a voice that seemed to be coming from the front yard. She went out into the yard. There was no one in sight. But when she turned to go back into the house, something caused her to look up. There, perched precariously on the side of the roof, was her baby. She had knocked out the screen, climbed out of the window and sat looking down at Nancy. It seemed that once again, Grandma Sophie had had a hand in helping the family avoid disaster.

Nancy claimed that whenever one of her children was ill, she felt the presence of another person in the house. Pete claimed to have seen a figure he believed to be the ghost of his mother standing by his son's bed, though it vanished as he entered the room. The parents said it seemed almost as if the children's grandmother were a kind of guardian angel.

Over the years, Nancy has learned to be more attentive to this spirit. One day she felt it beckoning her to follow. When she did, she discovered her six-year-old son and a playmate out behind the garage attempting to light some cigarettes. They might have been able to hide their antics from her, but not from Grandma Sophie!

Today this family, like others that are haunted, often hears creaking stairs or senses someone in the room with them. But where other families might want to be rid of their ghosts, Pete and Nancy hope theirs will never leave.

The Little Girl Who Wasn't There

The Clark family had moved into their large old house on Warren Avenue in Detroit when their youngest child, Rachel, was not yet three years old.

Even before the family had completely settled into the new home, Rachel announced that she had a little friend. She said her friend's name was Kenny Cobb. When her mother said she would like to meet him, Rachel explained that Kenny was a girl, not a boy, and that she was standing right beside her. Naturally, Mrs. Clark had heard of children having imaginary playmates, but she wondered how her daughter had happened to make up such a strange name.

Kenny Cobb soon became part of the household. Although only Rachel could see her, she kept the family well informed about everything Kenny said or did. Rachel's parents did not discourage Rachel since they had read that it was quite natural for a child to invent such a playmate and that it was, in fact, a sign of higher intelligence.

Rachel and Kenny Cobb remained friends for more than two years. Then, about a month after Rachel started kindergarten, her mother found her crying and asked what was wrong. Rachel announced that Kenny had come to say goodbye. It seemed that Kenny had told her that since Rachel now had other children to play with, it was time for Kenny to go.

As time went by, Rachel talked less and less about Kenny and the Clarks eventually forgot all about the little blonde-haired girl they had never seen.

Years passed, and Rachel had grown into a young woman when one night the Clarks attended a party on the other side of town. There they met several people they had never known before. When the Clarks mentioned where they lived, an older woman spoke up and said that many years ago she had lived in the same neighborhood.

"Exactly which house do you live in?" she asked.

The Clarks described their home, and she said, "Oh, yes, the old Cobb house. The Cobb family built that house but they didn't live there very long. They moved away right after their granddaughter was hit by a car and killed in front of the house."

The Clarks gasped at the name, Cobb. "What was the child's first name?" they both asked quickly.

"I can't remember," the woman replied, "but it was a boy's name. They called her by a boy's name — Billy, Bobby, Kenny, or something like that."

The Clarks looked at each other in astonishment. Rachel had not made it all up. She really had been playing with the ghost of Kenny Cobb.

The Clarks no longer live on Warren Avenue. Rachel is married now and has children of her own. But she feels certain that if ever another lonely little girl lives in the old Cobb house, Kenny will come back to keep her company until she finds new playmates.

VIII

Ghosts With a Purpose

Many ghosts worry about those they loved in life and had to leave behind. Several people have told me that a week or two after the death of a loved one, the beloved person has appeared to them in a dream, asserting that he or she is not really dead but is in fact well and happy.

This has happened so often to so many people that I do not believe it is a dream at all but an actual visit from a loved one who has returned to assure those left behind that all is as it should be. The message is important to those still living because it frees them to stop mourning and resume their own lives without guilt.

Other ghosts have left unfinished business and can't rest until it is attended to. Here is a collection of five stories about such ghosts. It seems they haunted in order to finish the unfinished or in some way to set matters straight for those left behind.

The Ghost of Mrs. Lowell

Mr. and Mrs. Lowell had lived in their comfortable little house in a small town in northeastern Michigan for more than 40 years. All five of their children had long since grown and gone out on their own. Mr. and Mrs. Lowell were enjoying their golden years in the same home they had moved into as newlyweds.

Then Mr. Lowell's health began to fail, and he was taken to a hospital. After a long illness, he died a welcome death. For the next five years, Mrs. Lowell continued to live in the house alone. Then she too died in the hospital, but of natural causes. Mrs. Lowell did not leave a formal will. What little she owned, including the house, was divided equally among her five children.

Neither of the Lowells, nor anyone else before them, had ever died in the house on Seventh Avenue.

None of the sons or daughters wanted to live in the house since they all had fine homes of their own. But neither did they want to sell it, for it held happy memories for each of them. Finally, they agreed to keep the house in the family and rent it out. And rent it they did! In the next two years, 13 families moved into and out of the house. All of the families left hurriedly and all for the same reason: the house, they claimed, was haunted. The last family to rent the house left at night. They called the owners to inform them, but refused to return to it even long enough to retrieve their furniture.

After hassling with renters, the Lowell family reluctantly decided it was best to sell the house. But that turned out to be easier said than done. In a town as small as theirs, news travelled fast. Everyone for miles around had heard of the ghost that lived there and no one wanted to buy a haunted house. So the once happy little home stood empty for nearly two years. During that time, the family shared the burden of cutting the grass, shoveling the snow, paying the taxes, and generally keeping the place up.

Not far away in a rented flat lived a young man named Ray Burton. He and his wife Emily had one child, Rebecca, who was as tall and graceful as a full grown woman although she was only 12 years old. The Burtons had never owned a home of their own. Robert Lowell knew that Ray's dream was to purchase a house for his little family, although on his meager salary he could barely afford the rent for the place where they lived. He had never been able to save enough money to make a down payment on even the most modest of houses. After discussing the Burtons with the rest of the family and gaining their approval, Robert offered to sell his parents' home to Ray Burton for half the market value of the property and without any down payment at all.

The Burtons had already heard the house was haunted, but they decided the Lowells had offered an opportunity too good to turn down. They would deal with the ghost if and when it appeared and not worry about it until then. The papers were soon signed and Ray, Emily, and Rebecca moved into their new home. The Lowells breathed a sigh of relief.

The Burtons had just settled in when, one night just after midnight, Emily awoke with a start. A figure wearing a long white night-gown was standing at the foot of her bed. Emily, still half-asleep, thought she was looking at her daughter. She spoke sharply asking, "Becky, what do you want? Whatever it is, can't it wait until morning? Go back to bed and let me sleep."

The figure turned and walked out of the room.

But Emily, by now fully awake, couldn't go back to sleep. When Becky came into her parent's room in the middle of the night, it was usually for a good reason. Perhaps the child was ill and really needed her. She went into Becky's room to apologize and find out what was troubling her daughter. But to her astonishment, she found Becky sound asleep in her own bed, wearing red and white striped pajamas. She certainly had not been the figure standing at the foot of Emily's bed in a white nightgown only moments before. Emily then knew the ghost of their haunted house had appeared and she had sent it away. But she knew without a doubt that it would soon return.

Ray and Emily had discussed ghosts on several occasions. They were both well read on the subject. They believed that when a departed spirit remained earthbound, it was because it had a message to deliver and it could not rest until that was accomplished. Sure enough, three nights later, the ethereal visitor appeared again at the foot of their bed. This time they were ready.

Ray was the first to see it and he quickly nudged Emily awake. As they had planned, Ray then spoke to the specter.

"Who are you?" he asked.

At first his inquiry was met with silence. He repeated the question.

At last the ghost spoke. Her voice was thin and shaky, but both Ray and Emily heard her clearly as she answered in little more than a whisper, "My name was Julia Lowell." Then stretching out her arm, she beckoned to them to follow her.

The house was completely dark, but an eerie light seemed to emanate from Julia's form. They could see her without difficulty as she led them toward the stairwell up to the attic. The house was a bungalow with two bedrooms and a large unframed attic. Sometime in the past, someone had laid a floor in the attic, but the walls and ceiling were still bare beams. The Burtons stored unpacked boxes there. Three folding cots and a roll-away bed, left behind by former tenants, suggested that the attic had probably been used as a bedroom, unfinished as it was. It had never been wired with electricity and contained no light fixtures. It was, in fact, just a dark, bleak, cavernous room.

Timidly the Burtons ascended the attic stairs led by the greenish-white light issuing from their ghostly visitor. When they reached the attic, Julia proceeded to the center of the room and pointed to a place in the far corner where the slanting roof met the floor. Then she vanished as suddenly as if someone had turned out a light.

Ray and Emily were left in total darkness, clutching each other in disbelief. Had this really happened, or had they dreamed it? Carefully, they felt their way down the stairs and turned on the lights below. As their courage began to return, they found a flashlight and gingerly reclimbed the attic stairs by its light.

Shining the light on the spot to which Julia had pointed, they saw nothing at first. Closer examination, however, revealed a space below the beams. Reaching into it, Ray pulled out an old-fashioned wooden cigar box that had been tucked beneath the rafters and hidden by the dust that covered room. It was bound by several rubber bands.

Returning downstairs to their brightly lit kitchen, they placed the box on the table and wiped away the dust. It didn't rattle when they shook it and it was not very heavy. They thought it probably held paper, perhaps important legal documents, or maybe even money. Ray's hands trembled as he removed the rubber bands and lifted the lid. Inside were five letters sealed in white envelopes now yellowed but still in good condition. There was one envelope addressed to each of Julia Lowell's five children. The Burtons did not open the envelopes or attempt to read their contents. Instead, early the next morning they delivered them to the people for whom they were intended.

Several years have now passed since that night. The Burtons still live in the house on Seventh Avenue, but never again has Julia visited them. It seems to them that Julia had written the letters to be read by her children after her death. While the letters went undiscovered, her spirit could not rest. But when at last they were found and delivered, Julia could rest in peace and haunt the house no more.

Papa Loves You

Carl Emmons was a retired policeman. He and his wife, Joyce, lived in a brand new condominium near Ann Arbor. Their children were grown and married and had families of their own. One of Carl's greatest joys in life was playing with his grandchildren.

To Joyce Emmons, life seemed almost too good to be true. She and Carl had always had a good marriage, even though there had been some hard years. Carl's salary as a policeman had not always been enough to meet their needs, and his job had been a dangerous one. She had learned to worry when he was even a few minutes late coming home. But now their debts were paid, their big old house was sold, and they had moved into a modern, bright little apartment. With Carl retired, they had more time together than ever before, and she was enjoying every minute of it.

One beautiful Saturday, Mike and Cathy brought the grandchildren over to visit while they went shopping. Carl laughed and rough-housed with little Jeffy, and Joyce had delighted in rocking Missy and singing to her.

After the children had gone home with their parents, Joyce fixed a light supper for Carl and herself. Then she went into the kitchen to do the dishes.

Carl went into the bedroom and shot himself.

Joyce's world was shattered. Not only had she lost her husband who had been the love of her life, she had lost her faith in his love. She had always believed that Carl loved her and was as happy with their life together as she was. Now she began to wonder: wouldn't a man have to be terribly unhappy to take his own life?

The children tried their best, but nothing they could do or say would console her. A month after Carl's death, she was no better; she ate little, spoke hardly at all, and seemed to have no interest in life.

And then Carl came back.

Twice she thought she had seen him sitting on her bed as she came into her room. Both times he seemed to vanish, leaving her unsure about what she had seen. Could she be losing her mind? She did not tell the children.

Then one evening Carl made another visit. Her children were all present, along with their husbands and wives. Carl appeared in the center of the room where they were sitting. Each of them saw him, and each heard him speak.

Looking at his wife and children, he spoke haltingly. "It was an accident," he said. "I was getting ready to clean the gun. The yellow ruler . . . ." His voice trailed off, and as he disappeared there was no mistaking his words, "Papa loves you."

Joyce dissolved into tears. How could she have been so foolish? Although Carl's years as a policeman were over, he still kept his gun loaded and ready, just as he had always done. And, out of habit, he had cleaned it as often as ever. On the night of his death, he had taken the gun out to clean it. Then he had spied a yellow plastic ruler on the floor where his grandson had left it. As he bent to pick up the ruler, the gun had gone off. And Joyce finally knew: it had been an accident all along.

Carl's ghost never visited the family again. But today Joyce is no longer despondent. She is certain once again that her husband loves her and is waiting somewhere for her to join him.

The Unkept Promise

Donald Montgomery, a Birmingham businessman, was only 61, but he was dying.

Donald had worked hard and successfully to provide a comfortable life for his wife Margaret and their daughter Anne. A pillar in his community, an honest businessman, a church usher, and a devoted husband and father, he had earned the love and respect of all who knew him. Although not a rich man, he had put his financial affairs in order, making certain that neither Margaret nor Anne would have to worry about money after his death.

As Donald lived out his last days, he knew that the secret he had been harboring for ten years could no longer remain his alone.

Ten years earlier Donald had become infatuated with a woman 25 years his junior. But he continued to love his wife, and he certainly didn't want to endanger his marriage, but neither did he want to stop thinking about and being with Sherry. Their affair lasted less than three months, and then they agreed that it was over. However, a week later, Sherry discovered that she was pregnant.

Sherry was a sensible person and did not want to marry Donald. The difference in their ages was not the only obstacle, nor would it have been even if Donald had been single. She knew in fact that the only thing they had ever really had in common was their physical attraction for each other, and that had already worn thin. But Sherry didn't want to cause trouble for Donald either. What she did want was the child. They talked it over together for several days and at last reached an agreement. Donald purchased a small house for Sherry in Grand Rapids, 150 miles away, into which she moved four months before her child was to be born. Posing as a widow, she found work and began a new life.

Keeping his promise, Donald sent a reasonable amount of money each month to help support of the child. Both he and Sherry felt it would be best for all concerned if he played no other part in the child's life. He never saw the baby, nor ever knew when it was born or whether it was a boy or girl. Now there was nothing to connect them in any way, except for the monthly money orders; Donald always signed those with a fictitious name. Sherry kept her part of the bargain and never attempted to contact him. The secret remained well hidden.

Never again did Donald stray from his marital bed. But he carried an overpowering burden of guilt. Many times, he had wanted to tell Margaret the whole story and relieve himself of the secret; but each time, he had realized that this would be a selfish thing to do. Although it would have eased his own conscience, it would only have served to devastate Margaret.

Being a conscientious man, Donald often worried about what would happen to the child if he died and his monthly money orders suddenly stopped coming. He did not dare to set up a trust fund or leave money in his will. Either of these would reveal the secret and break his wife's heart.

At last he hit upon a plan.

While still in good health, Donald took out an insurance policy payable upon his death to his daughter, Anne, who was already 28 years old, married, and the mother of children of her own. Anne and her family, along with her mother, had already been well provided for in Donald's will. And he had other life insurance policies from which Margaret would benefit. The new policy of course was really meant for Sherry's child. He knew that some day, before his death, he would have to confide in Anne and explain the situation. He would have to trust her not to hurt her mother by revealing his shameful secret.

Now the time had come when he could put it off no longer; his illness was terminal. A few days before his death, he summoned his daughter to his bedside. Explaining the affair and the child, he asked Anne to collect the insurance money and arrange for it to be given to Sherry and their child without Margaret's knowledge. Anne was devastated. Was this the father she had always loved and trusted? Still, common sense prevailed and she agreed to keep the story to herself and save her mother from pain. She promised her father, on his death bed, that she would do as he asked and see that the money went to her half-brother or sister without anyone else's knowledge.

Donald died at peace.

But after her father's death, Anne was bitter. She found she could not forgive him. She cashed the policy but made no attempt to locate the child for whom the money was intended. Instead, she deposited it in an account in her own name. She didn't need the money. In addition to the inheritance her father had bequeathed her, she and her husband already owned a comfortable home and had savings of their own. The insurance money sat in the bank accumulating interest and Anne put the matter out of her mind.

Nearly four years passed. One afternoon, while Anne's children were in school and her husband was at work, she went to the supermarket to do her weekly grocery shopping.

Pushing her shopping cart along the aisles she made her selections. But as she reached for a bottle of vinegar from the shelf, there was her father suddenly standing before her. Looking into her eyes he said, "Anne, you didn't keep your promise."

Anne let out a startled scream, dropped the vinegar, and rushed from the store, leaving her grocery cart standing in the aisle. She sat in her car in the parking lot trembling with fear and embarrassment. Was her mind playing tricks on her? She couldn't have seen her father's ghost, could she? Such things just didn't happen. She felt she would never be able to shop in that store again.

Slowly, regaining her composure, she drove home without her groceries. She told no one what had happened. The next day, Anne went shopping in another market. All went well, and a week passed uneventfully.

Then one evening, Anne's family was assembled in the living room. Her husband was reading the paper, the children were watching television, and she was busy knitting an afghan as a Christmas gift for her mother-in-law. Suddenly the front door flew open and in walked Donald Montgomery. He stood in the center of the room, looked directly at his daughter, and said in a sorrowful voice, "Annie, you didn't keep your promise."

Anne's husband and children had all seen the door burst open, but they insisted it had been blown open by the wind. None of them saw Donald or heard his voice, and none of them understood why Anne became suddenly so upset. After calming down, Anne decided that she had just been on edge.

It took a third incident to convince her.

The following Sunday, she and her family attended church in Bloomfield Hills as they did every week. Her husband was singing in the choir, and she and the children were seated in their usual pew. The collection basket came down the row. Anne, seated on the aisle, placed her envelope on top of the others and began to hand the basket to the waiting usher. Looking up, she discovered not the usher but her father standing there with his hand outstretched toward her. She collapsed in a dead faint.

Anne confided in no one. But Monday morning when the bank opened she was the first in line. Withdrawing the insurance money and the interest it had earned, she set off across the state to reach the address her father had given her before his death.

By noon, she had located Sherry.

Sherry told her the child, a girl, was now nearly 14 years old. She showed Anne a picture. The girl reminded Anne of herself at that age. Sherry had married and had had two more children. Her husband treated Donald's child as he did his own. They were a happy family.

Naturally, Sherry had been disappointed when the money orders had stopped coming four years earlier, but she assumed that Donald had died or had been unable, for some other reason, to send them. She had known he was a man of his word. She had made no attempt to contact him, having promised him that she would never bring grief to his wife.

Anne felt a twinge of guilt. Sherry had been much better at keeping a promise than she herself had. She handed the money to Sherry knowing that it would indeed be used just as her father had intended it. Then the two women agreed that someday, when Margaret was no longer living, Anne and the girl would meet.

Returning home late that afternoon, Anne felt that a great burden had been lifted from her shoulders. She wished that she could see her father one more time to tell him that she was sorry she hadn't kept her promise sooner. But Donald Montgomery never visited his daughter again. Now at last, he could truly rest in peace.

The Jingling Keys

Esther Suttle was a hard-working, conscientious woman. She and her husband George had been employed for 27 years as housekeepers in a well-known Grosse Pointe home.

George had died several years before and Esther had wanted to retire, but the family she worked for convinced her that she was indispensable. Although she could no longer do any heavy cleaning, or even be on her feet for very long, her mere presence in the house seemed to keep things running smoothly. She directed the work of the younger employees and made sure that everything was done as it should be.

Esther and George had had only one child, a girl. She had died young, leaving behind a baby daughter named Nancy. Nancy herself was now married with a family of her own, and lived in a neat little house in East Detroit.

Although she lived in the house where she worked in Grosse Pointe, Esther spent more and more time at her granddaughter's home after George's death. She would often ride the bus to East Detroit after work and stay overnight. Rising early in the morning, she would be back at work in time to see that breakfast was properly served.

On one particular night, Esther spent the evening as usual with Nancy's family. They talked, watched television, and had a cup of tea before going to bed. Esther kissed them all goodnight and climbed the stairs to her room. That night, she died peacefully in her sleep.

Nancy knew that her grandmother had had a long and happy life and that it was her time to go. But Esther had held a very special place in Nancy's heart, and her death was a great loss. In Esther's old room, Nancy found she could not bear to sort out her grandmother's things just then. So she left the room as it was and closed the door. But as she walked down the stairs, she heard what sounded like keys jingling. She felt it was probably her imagination.

Later that evening, after Nancy and her husband had returned from making arrangements at the funeral parlor, she again heard the jingling sound. She mentioned it to her husband, but he had not heard it. Twice in the night she heard the sound. When she couldn't go back to sleep, Nancy went downstairs to fix herself a cup of tea. And there in the doorway to the kitchen stood Grandma Esther, shaking her key ring violently. Nancy's screams awoke her husband and he rushed downstairs. He tried to comfort her, telling her that she had been through a terrible ordeal that day and it was only natural that her nerves were causing her to see things that weren't there. Nancy supposed he was right and hoped that she wasn't losing her mind.

The next day the relatives began arriving from out of town. Nancy busied herself making everyone else comfortable. Although she thought she heard the jingling once or twice, no one else seemed to notice it so she said nothing. But as everyone was preparing to go to the funeral home, Nancy looked up and saw her grandmother coming toward her, shaking her key ring wildly in Nancy's face. Nancy began to cry uncontrollably. Blaming her outburst on her grief, the family comforted her on the way to the funeral parlor. Nancy finally regained her composure and sat quietly in the mourner's room, speaking politely when spoken to. But as they prepared to leave for the night, Nancy froze in horror.

Grandma was getting up out of her coffin. But no one else seemed to notice!

Nancy looked more closely. Her grandmother's body was still lying in the casket, but there was Grandma now standing beside her shaking those jingling keys. Nancy ran out of the room, screaming. Her husband caught up with her in the parking lot and held her. "Get hold of yourself girl," he urged. "I know you loved her, but you can't go on acting this way."

Nancy tried to explain about the keys. He asked if she had ever seen the keys before.

"Why, yes," she told him. "They're the keys to the house where she worked. Grandma always carried them."

"Where are they now?" he asked.

"I don't know, but I suppose they're in her room," Nancy answered.

They drove home and went straight to Esther's room. The ring of keys was lying on the dresser where Esther had put them before going to bed for the last time. They decided that perhaps Esther was worried that the keys would fall into the wrong hands. So, not even waiting until morning, they took the keys to her former employer's home that very night.

Nancy never heard them jingle again.

Grandpa's Strong Box

For years, Barbara Lee and I worked together in the same school district, and at one time I was her son's second grade teacher. We have been close friends for nearly 30 years. When I told her that I was contemplating writing this book, she confided that she had a story to tell that would add to my collection. Although the events in this tale occurred many years ago, she still remembers them vividly. In fact, it is unlikely that she will ever forget what happened that night in Hazel Park.

Back in the 1930s, Barbara's grandfather lost a small savings account when the banks closed suddenly, leaving him and thousands of others across the nation unable to withdraw their money. From then on, he never again trusted banks and kept all his money and important papers hidden in his house.

Nana, as Barbara called her grandmother, was an old fashioned sort of woman who did not work outside of her home, did not drive a car, and left the bill-paying to her husband. She had never worried about money, for as far as she was concerned it was her husband's job to handle the financial matters. He was a good, hard-working, conscientious man, and she had never doubted that he would always provide well for her.

Their home in Hazel Park was completely paid for. There were two good-sized insurance policies listing Nana as beneficiary and there was a tidy sum of money put aside from her husband's many years of hard work and careful saving. The problem was that Nana could not prove any of this. The deed to the house, the insurance papers, and the cash were all safely stored in a metal strong box. But the old man had died suddenly without ever telling his wife where he had put it.

Nana missed her husband painfully. And now, in addition to her grief, she had no money. Six weeks had gone by since her husband's death and she still had not found the strong box. Without the proper papers, she could not claim any insurance. Even the undertaker was still unpaid. Nana reluctantly accepted money from her children even to buy groceries.

Everyone in the family had tried to find the box. They had cleaned out cupboards, closets, and trunks. They had looked for false bottoms or secret compartments in the desk, dressers, and bureaus. They had thoroughly searched every nook and cranny from the attic to the basement, but to no avail.

After one particularly frustrating day, Nana asked Barbara and her little son Corky to spend the night since she didn't want to be alone. Barbara, of course, accepted and since they were very tired, all three went to bed early. Barbara and her little boy occupied the bedroom next to Nana's. There she could easily hear the older woman if she called out in the night.

Shortly after midnight, Barbara was awakened by the sounds of talking that seemed to be coming from her grandmother's room. Getting out of bed, she went to Nana's room and tapped softly on the door. Her grandmother opened it at once and, smiling broadly, she invited Barbara to come in. Barbara fully expected to see one of her relatives there for she was certain she had heard Nana talking to someone just a moment before. But there was no one else in the room. Nana, however, was very excited.

"Barbara," she exclaimed, "your grandfather was just here and we had the nicest visit."

"You were dreaming, Nana," Barbara told her.

But the older woman insisted that it hadn't been a dream. She said that her husband had come back to tell her that everything was all right and that she should not worry. He said they would be together again someday. But Barbara was worried, afraid Nana had gone a little daft from grief and stress. She decided to call one of her aunts to come at once.

"Don't you go near that phone," ordered her grandmother. "Just bring me a hammer and a chisel and hurry."

Surprised, Barbara decided to humor her. She went and got the tools and brought them back to the bedroom, where she was puzzled to find the rug rolled back and her grandmother down on all fours counting the floor boards. Suddenly Nana patted a spot that looked no different than the rest of the floor.

"Pry up these boards at once," she told Barbara.

To Barbara's amazement, the boards lifted easily, and there, at last, was the long-hidden metal strong box. Taking it from its hiding place, she handed it to her grandmother, who quickly opened it. Inside were the long sought papers, and nearly five thousand dollars in cash.

Nana began crying, not tears of sorrow but tears of joy. She said she had been awakened from her restless sleep by someone calling her name. As she turned in her bed she had seen her husband standing near her.

"He was real," she insisted, "as real as you are."

She said he had sat down on the bed beside her and they had talked for a long time. He had told her where to find the box, but they had also talked about many other things as well. Then he had said goodbye and kissed her cheek before disappearing just as Barbara knocked at the door.

Barbara does not often tell this story for fear people will think she is balmy. But since then, she has never doubted the existence of ghosts.

IX

Automatic Writing
(Ouija Boards, Planchettes, and Just Plain Pen and Paper)

Almost everyone is familiar with the Ouija, a flat board 18 by 12 inches, with the alphabet and the words "yes," "no," and "goodbye" printed on it. It is used with a pointer. The name "Ouija" comes from the French and German words "oui" and "ja" meaning yes. A planchette is a small wooden instrument, usually triangular or heart-shaped, mounted on ball bearing casters and very much like the pointer used with the Ouija board. A pencil or ballpoint pen is inserted in the planchette so that it writes messages instead of merely pointing out letters as the Ouija pointer does. Both of these items are tools for automatic writing through which we can receive messages.

I prefer the planchette over the Ouija board for two reasons. A Ouija board must be used by two players. I can't be completely certain that the other player isn't pushing the pointer and influencing the message, and I'm sure that at times the other player has similar doubts about me. Also, the pointer on the Ouija board often moves very fast and, human memory being what it is, the message may not always be recalled accurately when you are trying to analyze it later. On the other hand, the planchette is used by only one person. If it moves, either you or some outside force is pushing it; and, you have a written record of the message.

Whether or not you believe these messages, there is no disputing the fact that they appear. The question is, where do they come from? Are they really from deep within your mind? Is the instrument you're using being pushed by other forces? And are the messages you get the words of other entities — spirits dwelling on another plane?

In 1979, I conducted a non-credit class on understanding automatic writing in the College of Continuing Education at Wayne State University. One of my students, a gentle old man in his 70s, insisted that the writing his planchette produced was the work of a ghost. When I asked him why he was so certain, he answered, "All it ever writes is dirty words, and I don't talk that way!" I really don't believe that old man ever did say a dirty word, but his planchette may have provided a way for his subconscious to express such thoughts and put the blame on a ghost.

When people use either the Ouija board or the planchette, it is not uncommon for the boards to express all sorts of obscenities and oaths, things the individuals using it would never dream of saying aloud, at least not consciously. I hasten to point out that people are usually not conscious of the fact that they are producing these words and thoughts themselves. They really believe they're seeing the work of an evil spirit and are often frightened by it. Nevertheless, controlling the pointer or planchette gives them a wonderful opportunity to rid themselves of their pent-up anger and blame it on an evil spirit.

This doesn't mean a ghost couldn't give you a message in this way. If you feel a spirit has been trying to contact you, you could perhaps help it by sitting in the haunted area with a planchette. Some people claim to receive inspired writing using nothing more than an ordinary pen and paper. Others have been able to type out whole manuscripts. One woman writes scores for musical compositions which she believes are given to her by Liszt, Mozart, and other long dead composers. Many of the things people write in this way are pure fantasy, of course, much like dreams. They should be accepted as such and be interpreted in the same way as dreams your mind creates while you are sleeping.

It sometimes happens, though, that a user of the Ouija or planchette really is a very clairvoyant person who can discover things by using a pointer or planchette to help channel their clairvoyance. Take the case of Delores and her neighbor, for instance.

Delores was a reformed gambler. Before she finally agreed to therapy that eventually helped her control her habit, she had lost thousands of dollars and had run up debts that forced her husband into bankruptcy. But now it had been over five years since she had gone to the tracks, played cards, or even purchased a one-dollar lottery ticket. Her husband had stood by her through her recovery and to celebrate her fifth anniversary of abstinence, he gave her a beautiful diamond ring to replace the engagement and wedding ring set she had once sold for gambling money. The stones in her new ring were not large, but the ring could not have meant more to her if it had been the Hope Diamond. It represented her husband's continuing love and renewed faith in her.

One day she misplaced the ring. She had taken it off while doing housework and could not remember where she had put it. Frantically she searched the house, but it was nowhere to be found. Her next door neighbor dropped by to visit and found her crying. Delores told her the story and said that if she did not find the ring before her husband came home — and he noticed that she wasn't wearing it — she was afraid he would think she was gambling again.

The neighbor told her to get some paper and sit across from her at the kitchen table. Then, from her purse, she took out a wooden planchette. She told Delores to sit and relax as she placed the planchette on the paper and lightly touched it with her finger tips. Before long, the heart-shaped instrument began to move. At first it produced little more than just scribbles and then it wrote the word "pillbox." Delores remembered at once that she had put the ring in a little pillbox in her jewelry case.

How had the neighbor done this? I doubt that any spirits were involved. I believe that in this case the neighbor herself didn't know how she had done it; still, she managed to tap into Delores' subconscious mind where the secret was hidden.

In the stories that follow, messages come from two very different sources. Fujar is a poltergeist produced by the energy and imaginations of two teenage girls. In the second tale, however, the message comes from a real ghost who guides Dottie's hand as she writes with a planchette.

Fujar

Mr. and Mrs. Freeland made plans to take a short trip, leaving Kelly, their 16-year-old daughter, at home overnight without them for the first time. Kelly's best friend Lori would stay with her. The doors were to be kept locked and no other visitors allowed in the house until the Freelands returned home the next day.

This suited the girls because they were planning to conduct a very serious experiment. A few weeks earlier, Lori had found an old Ouija board the neighbors had put out for the trash collector. She and Kelly had been waiting for an opportunity to try it. There were no instructions with it, but a book from the library told the girls how to use it and how to protect themselves from evil spirits as well.

After Kelly's parents had left and the girls had finished off the pizza they had ordered for supper, they prepared the living room for the evening's adventure. They decided to use the coffee table to support the board rather than trying to balance it on their knees, and they arranged pillows on the floor to sit on. On the table, they placed the Ouija board and a wine glass to use as a pointer since they hadn't found the one that belonged with the board. Next to these, they placed a crucifix Lori had taken from the wall in the spare bedroom of her grandmother's house, and two candles prepared according to the book's direction: a black one anointed with conjuring oil and a white one dressed with protection oil.

Shopping for the oils a week before had been an adventure in itself. They had found a place to buy their supplies through the Greater Detroit Yellow Pages. After much pleading and coaxing, they had convinced Lori's uncle to take them to an occult shop near the New Center area of town. The Goodwill Candle Shop, also known as the "House of a Thousand Candles," was (and still is, I believe) the largest over-the-counter store of its kind anywhere in the country and, perhaps, in the world. It resembled a supermarket. The girls were fascinated with the Black Cat candles, oils, incenses, and potions, the likes of which they had never seen before. They found and bought what they needed. (Kelly also purchased a small envelope of true love powder. She wasn't sure when or how she would use it, but thought it might be a good thing to have on hand just in case she needed it someday.)

When everything was ready, they drew the drapes, lit the treated candles, and seated themselves on either side of the low table. Turning the wine class upside down on the center of the board, they placed their fingertips on its pedestal base. Thus began an experience they would long remember.

At first all was quiet. After a while, Kelly became restless and suggested that perhaps there weren't any spirits in that house. Lori said that she had read that spirits were everywhere and suggested they be patient.

"Well," exclaimed Kelly, "if there really are any spirits here, I wish they'd make themselves known!" The words were no sooner uttered than the wine glass began to move. It flew about the board without stopping at any letter. It finally came to rest at the top of the board on the word "Ouija." The girls began to question it and again the pointer moved in response.

Lori asked, "Is there really a spirit here?"

"Where do you come from?" asked Kelly.

The glass scooted from the moon to the sun and star and back again, then, covering one letter at a time it spelled out, "Nowhere and everywhere."

Lori asked, "Why are you here?"

The Ouija answered, "Because you called me."

This was great stuff! It was working better than they had dared hope for. Both girls were trembling with excitement. Kelly asked again, "Do you have a message for us?"

The glass glided to the word "Yes."

"What is it?" asked Lori.

The Ouija answered, "John loves Lori."

At this, Lori snatched her hand from the glass. Furious, she fairly screamed at Kelly, accusing her of pushing the glass to spell out that "dumb" message. "Can't you take anything seriously?" she demanded. "Are boys all you can think about?"

Kelly insisted she had neither pushed the glass nor directed its movement in any way. She accused Lori of pushing it herself since she was so nutty over John. But after arguing a bit more, they decided to try again and both swore that they would not force the glass to move.

This time, placing their fingers on the glass, they didn't have time to ask a question before it began to move about and spell out the words "Stupid females!" Not knowing whether to laugh or be angry, Lori asked, "Who are you?"

The Ouija answered, "My name is Fujar." And, after a short pause, it asked the girls, "Will you help me?" Answering together, they agreed and asked what Fujar wanted them to do.

"Find Nina Evans," spelled out the pointer.

Neither Kelly nor Lori had ever heard the name before and one of them asked who this person was and how they could find her. The board repeated itself again and again, "Find Nina Evans, Nina Evans, Nina Evans," moving faster and faster. Then fairly flying around the board, the glass began to spell out wild unconnected words: "tabernacle, horses, over, under, upside down, Nina Evans, pigsty, porcupine, big book," and other words the girls could not decipher. They began to be frightened when suddenly the messages changed and the glass spelled out a string of obscenities and then " . . . kill, blood, blood on the door, blood on your hands . . . " followed by more obscenities.

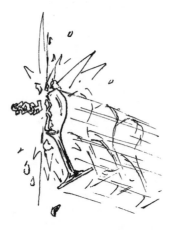

Both girls suddenly screamed as the glass left their hands and flew off the table as if it had been thrown. It crashed into the wall across the room and shattered. A picture fell from the wall and a lamp tipped over. Lori grabbed the crucifix and held it high up in the air. Rapping and thumping noises filled the room. The furniture began shaking as if they were in the midst of an earthquake. Lori's hands were cut and bleeding and there was a smudge of fresh blood on the door leading into the next room.

It was several minutes before the noises and shaking finally stopped.

The girls clung to each other crying hysterically. Later, having finally regained their composure, they cleaned up the broken glass and returned things to their proper places. Neither girl slept that night, although the house remained quiet.

To this day, Fujar has never returned. But then, neither girl has ever again played with the Ouija.

Getting It All Back Together Again

No one was surprised when the Richters decided to live in an old barn in Washtenaw County.

They were the kind of people who would have been quite out of place in an ordinary house. Lyle was an architect, and Dottie had just left her job teaching art at Eastern Michigan University to begin free-lance work. Together they turned their talents and their savings to converting their barn into a dream house.

The building was structurally sound but required a huge amount of electrical work and plumbing. They kept the outside of the barn as natural looking as possible, while inside they allowed their imaginations to run wild. Lyle designed a circular stairway that wound up through an old silo at one end of the building; it led to bedrooms in what had once been the hayloft.

During the remodeling, the couple slept on cots on the main floor. Not until the last nail was hammered in, the last curtain hung, and the last piece of furniture put into place did they finally move upstairs to the largest of the loft bedrooms. Exhausted from their efforts, but proud and happy with the results of the months and months of work, they decided to celebrate by opening a bottle of champagne. They drank toasts to their happiness and talked far into the night about the open house party they would throw to show off their new home.

They had been asleep only a short time when suddenly, just before dawn, they awoke to find a man, dressed in farm clothes, standing at the foot of their bed. They didn't have time to speak out before he vanished into the shadows. The room was only dimly lit by the pre-dawn light. Lyle turned on a lamp, but their visitor was gone. They searched the house but found no one and nothing seemed to have been disturbed. They decided that they must have seen someone who had come in merely to look, but not to wake them or do any harm. Still, the following night, they made sure that the doors were bolted securely before they went to bed.

Again, just before dawn, Dottie awoke with a sense that someone was in their room. She shook Lyle to wake him. He didn't see anyone or feel anything strange. They decided that Dottie had just become nervous because of the visitor the night before. But before long it became evident that something very strange was indeed happening. Every morning without fail, just before dawn, either Lyle or Dottie, sometimes both, would be awakened by some undefinable presence. Twice Lyle again saw the figure that had first visited. Both times, it had vanished without a word.

Finally Dottie decided to try an experiment. She had read about automatic or spirit writing and decided to try to communicate with their visitor with the help of a planchette. She obtained one of the little heart-shaped boards from a friend. The following morning she awoke long before day break and sat at a little table in the bedroom. She positioned the planchette with ball bearing rollers and a ball point pen on a piece of clean white paper and placed her fingers lightly on top of the board. Almost immediately it began to write, though at first only in a scribble. Dottie became sure she was making contact with a force other than human.

"Who are you?" she asked. The planchette darted across the paper and spelled out, "My name was Luther Cooke." Dottie read the words and squealed with delight, "Lyle, Lyle, wake up! He's here!"

Lyle examined the paper and agreed that it was certainly not Dottie's handwriting that appeared there. But he was not convinced that a ghost had written it either. He asked her to try again, and again she placed her fingers on the board and waited. Nothing happened. But Dottie had had some success with the planchette already and she refused to give up. Every morning she awoke just before sunrise and sat ready for her visitor. At last, five days later, her patience was rewarded. She felt the board begin to move almost as soon as she touched it. Through her questions, she obtained the following story.

It seemed that Luther Cooke was a migrant farm hand who had

come there to work during the summer of 1906. At the end of the season's work, he had quarreled with the farmer over wages, and a bloody fight had ensued in the very barn where Lyle and Dottie now lived. The farmer had grabbed an axe and before killing Luther he had severed Luther's hand from his wrist. In his haste to bury Luther's body, the farmer had overlooked the hand until he returned to clean up the murder site. Then, instead of burying the hand behind the barn with the rest of the body, he dug a hole and buried it beneath the back steps of the farm house. Luther's ghost seemed obsessed with the desire to have all of his body parts together again. He begged Dottie to find his hand and place it in the grave with the rest of his bones.

In utter disbelief, Lyle read what the planchette had written. To satisfy his wife, he agreed to try to find the two burial spots.

Like many Michigan farmers, the original owner of the property had invested far more time, money, and effort in building a good barn for his cows than a good house for his wife. The old farmhouse had fallen down or been demolished long since. However, there was evidence of where it had once stood and it was not difficult to sur-mise the location of the back steps. Lyle had been digging there for a few minutes before he found a number of small bones which might possibly be those from a human hand. Dottie brought out pots and strainers and they sifted the earth thoroughly so as not to leave even one small bone behind. They placed the bones carefully in a small box and then began the search for the main grave. Their digging behind the barn continued for two days. Lyle was about to abandon the search when the white bone of a skull appeared under the shovel.

Lyle considered calling the police to report his discovery, but Dottie pointed out that nothing would be gained by it since everyone connected with the murder had long since died. So, saying nothing to the authorities, they placed the bones of the hand in the grave with the skull and covered it over again.

From then on, Luther Cooke appeared no more. The Richters believe he was satisfied that he had finally gotten himself back together.

X

Haunted Houses

In 1983, I lectured a group of women at the public library in Plymouth, Michigan, on the subject of haunts and hauntings. It was my custom, after such a lecture to invite members of the audience to share with me their own experiences with ghosts. On that particular night in 1983, Arlene, a Northville grandmother and lifelong resident of the area, told me about a restaurant that she believed to be haunted. Her story began 40 years ago, when the building housing the restaurant was a private home.

Arlene remembers her first visits to the magnificent mansion on Nine Mile Road just west of Haggerty in Novi, Michigan. Arlene's best friend, Mary Ellen Crusoe, lived in the fine old house at the time, and Arlene was a frequent visitor there.

One day, while the two girls were talking quietly in the south end of the library, the glass covering a large picture at the opposite end of the room suddenly shattered and fell to the floor. A startled butler rushed into the room, surveyed the damage, and angrily accused the girls of causing it. They, of course, knew themselves to be innocent. But on other occasions Arlene and Mary Ellen were accused of turning lights on and off, opening and closing doors, and making strange noises on the back stairs. Arlene recalled that whenever she walked up or down the main stairway, she felt that someone unseen was watching her. She had been certain, even then, that the house was haunted. And now, having had lunch in the mansion — now converted to a restaurant — her feelings about it remained unchanged.

I decided to visit the place myself and see what more I could learn. I soon became acquainted with the owner and several of the employees, all of whom clearly shared Arlene's opinion.

Home Sweet Home

A combination of 1920s New England and Old Southern Georgian architecture, the gracious house had been built in 1929 by Charles Rogers for his bride, the former Harriet Thornton, on the site of the original Thornton homestead.

The old farmhouse where Harriet's parents lived had been moved to make way for the grand new house. (The farmhouse still stands just northeast of the mansion.) At one time, the two houses had been joined by a secret underground tunnel which was later closed off and sealed up.

Charles Rogers' family had made a fortune in the canned milk industry and are still credited with the invention of condensed milk. The beautiful Rogers home was often referred to as the "White House Manor" not only because of its color but because it was paid for by the profits from the White House Milk Company. Always a showplace, it had towering columns, fabulous balconies, and a picturesque wishing well. It featured pediments, pilasters, and cornices outside, and hand-carved woodwork, thick rich paneling, and sculpted ceilings inside. Beveled, leaded, glass doors and stained glass windows added to the grandeur.

The most arresting feature of all was the home's grand staircase in the entrance hall. Ten feet wide, the stairs had cherry wood banisters that curved elegantly upward to encircle the entire second floor. Rogers had built this stairway for the daughter he had hoped to have, dreaming of leading her down those stairs on her wedding day. It was a dream that never came true, for although he and his wife were blessed with four fine sons, they never had a daughter.

But there was, at last, a granddaughter! And the day she announced her engagement, Charles began at once to plan the wedding. No expense would be spared. The entire house was redecorated. Flowers graced the entryway and every mantle and, of course, the staircase. Chefs worked for days to prepare a banquet unlike any other. All was made ready for the joyful day when Charles would escort his granddaughter down the stairs to her waiting bridegroom.

Alas, on the very eve of the wedding, the young couple eloped.

Shortly thereafter, on November 11, 1942, Charles Rogers died of a broken heart. His body lay in state in the great hall at the foot of his magnificent stairway.

After her husband's death, Harriet Rogers continued to live on in the grand old home until her own death. Her casket was placed, not in the great hall, but in the library — at the north end of the room by the very wall where Arlene and her friend Mary Ellen were to see the picture glass break years later.

After Mrs. Rogers' death, the house was occupied by the Crusoe family for about ten years, and then by a family named Sincolas who lived there until 1973. For the next several years, the house stood empty.

Then in 1981, the Cervi brothers bought the house and converted it into an elegant restaurant. They named it "The White House Manor," reviving the mansion's old unofficial name. The Cervi's were careful to keep the building's sedate atmosphere. They carefully decorated it in ways that they were sure would have pleased Charles Rogers. Using patterned wall fabrics, plush carpeting, and velvet draperies, they restored the house's former elegance.

Mike Cervi, manager and co-owner, loved the old mansion, but soon realized that along with the building had come at least one ghost, possibly two. Late at night, after everyone else had gone home and Mike was alone in the mansion, he would hear footsteps on the stairs, or doors opening and closing. On several different nights, he had carefully turned out the lights before locking up only to see them go on again once he had reached his car in the parking lot. Other people told him they had seen lights on the unused third floor when no one was in the building. But a close examination of the third floor never revealed anything but dust.

Women customers began to report strange experiences in the ladies' room on the second floor — the bathroom once joined to the master bedroom. One woman insisted that she had heard someone moving about in the toilet stall. The toilet flushed, she said, but no one came out. After waiting for some time, she gently touched the door. It swung open, and the stall was empty. Other patrons described similar experiences.

Sherry, who tended bar in the restaurant, reported that she had been frightened out of her wits the first time the huge mirror hanging over the bar shattered when no one was anywhere near it. After it was replaced, the same thing happened on two more occasions. And whole stacks of wine glasses would suddenly tumble over and go crashing to the floor behind the bar. I soon learned that the bar was located in the same spot where Harriet's casket had stood in the old library. The wall behind it was the same wall from which Arlene and Mary Ellen had seen the picture fall, 40 years earlier.

Before long, Sherry, like Arlene, became convinced that the house was haunted. One evening after the restaurant had closed for the night, someone had pinched her as she was climbing the main stairs. She distinctly heard a man chuckle softly right beside her. But there were only two other people in the building then and both were in the kitchen cleaning up. This left no doubt in Sherry's mind that the ghost was a man.

But others who worked in the mansion believed the ghost to be a woman. Richard Shank waited tables at the White House Manor and was affectionately known to his customers as "Captain Napkin." One day when the manager was nowhere in sight and Richard was alone in the bar, he decided to mix himself a drink. Suddenly he heard and felt someone standing beside him. He felt certain it was a woman, and could even smell her lavender perfume. She reached out and knocked the glass from his hand, and he clearly heard her shout "No."

It certainly seemed as though neither Charles nor Harriet was really willing to give the place up.

Ironically, in the short time (a little more than three years) that the restaurant was in business, more than 30 weddings were held on the grand staircase. I like to think that Charles Rogers stood nearby to witness them, still pining for the wedding he had longed for so many years ago.

In 1984, financial problems forced the Cervi brothers to close the White House Manor and once again it stood empty for a time. Then in 1987, its present owners, Steve Romanik and his sister, Suzi, redecorated and reopened it under a new name, "Home Sweet Home." It might well be unrecognizable to Charles and Harriet Rogers. Everything in the stately old place is now deliberately mismatched. Four different styles of chairs may sit around one table that matches not a one of them. The artwork is a conglomeration of paintings, photos, and sculptures from a variety of periods. All carpeting has been removed and the parquet floors have been painted with borders and designs. The stairway, too, is painted. In one room, the crystal chandelier has been replaced by one made of plumbing pipes. Electric candles flicker like Christmas tree lights throughout the building. Inside and out, everything is painted black and white.

But it seems that even this treatment of the old showplace has not dislodged Charles and Harriet Rogers.

One dark October night in 1988, after the diners had left and the doors were closed to the public, Steve Romanik and I, along with several news reporters, and perhaps 20 other people, held a seance in the mansion.

We arranged our chairs in a circle, sat down, and held hands. The flickering electric candles offered the only light. At first, all was quiet. Then suddenly several people went into trance-like states and began to babble. One woman fainted. The chandelier shook as if it were being blown about by a tornado. And although Steve Romanik and his employees insisted there was no one upstairs in the house, we clearly heard thumping, bumping noises coming from the second floor, as if furniture were being tossed about. However, when members of the group went upstairs to investigate, all seemed to be in perfect order.

There was a lot of activity in the house that night, but I don't believe that anyone there talked with Charles or Harriet.

Since that time, little has changed. Patrons of the restaurant, particularly women, complain of strange feelings on the main stairway. The second-floor ladies' room still seems to be occupied from time to time by an unseen user. Lights still turn on and off at late hours, and weird noises are still heard in the night. But all of this seems to have discouraged no one.

Arlene, who plans to continue eating there, still feels she is being watched and sometimes even followed. But she isn't frightened. "After all," she says, "they have never really hurt anybody, and it was their home first. I think they belong there."

It would seem that Charles and Harriet Rogers believe so, too.

The Remodeled House

In the strange tale that follows, a house began to be haunted only after it was remodeled. I visited there and spoke with several members of the Morton family. While nothing unusual took place during my visit, I believe the Mortons were telling the truth. Who or what caused the phenomena they experienced and why, I won't try to guess. I'll simply tell you the story as it was told to me.

Hal and Eleanor Morton purchased a small two-bedroom house on a tree-lined street in Livonia, and for five years, they and their children lived happily there. But as the children grew older, it became increasingly evident that the Morton family needed a larger home.

They really didn't want to move. They loved the area. The neighbors were all friendly, the children were happy in the school they attended, and they were conveniently located near good shopping centers. Although they had all the advantages of city living, they lived in a part of town that had maintained an almost rural atmosphere.

The people who owned the property before them had built an enormous garage behind the house. Mrs. Morton often remarked that nobody needed a garage that large, and wouldn't it be fine to have all that extra space inside the house. So, instead of moving, they built a new, smaller garage and connected the existing one to the house with a beautiful glass-enclosed breezeway. They then converted the old garage into a spectacular great room, at the same time remodeling the main part of the house. Walls were torn out and new partitions were built, bathrooms were added, and windows were replaced. When the work was completed, the house had become a showplace featuring a skylight, a fireplace, and a master bedroom with a dressing room and bath befitting a movie star.

But soon after the construction work was finished, odd things began to happen.

The dog, who had begun acting strangely, disappeared and never returned. The cat yowled and hissed at nothing at all, and one night, it ran screeching through the house and then dropped dead. The veterinary that examined the body said the cat had died of heart failure. After that, the Mortons seemed unable to keep any pet for more than a week or two. Every animal they brought home either ran away or became deathly ill.

Then one day while seated at the vanity in her beautiful new bathroom, Eleanor Morton noticed cat tracks on the tiles. It had been at least six months since they had had a cat. She washed the paw prints away, only to find that they reappeared the next day. To this day, the tracks have returned again and again, though no cat has ever been seen in the house.

And there have been other unexplained events.

Every so often, cold air will suddenly fill the great room, even when the fireplace flue is closed and there are no doors or windows open. The room is well-insulated and usually quite warm except when this occurs.

Occasionally, the overpowering smells of exotic perfume or pungent pipe tobacco will fill the house, although no one in the house uses either of these.

The strangest phenomenon of all happens on rainy nights. Since the house was remodeled, the Mortons have come to dread storms. Every rainy night at exactly midnight, the household is awakened by an urgent knocking at the side door, the one leading into the beautiful new breezeway. When the door is opened, no one is ever there.

One night, during a heavy rain, the Mortons decided to catch whoever was knocking. They pretended to go to bed as usual. Then after the lights were turned off, they sneaked back out of their bedrooms. Eleanor Morton unlatched the side door so that it could be flung open quickly. They took their positions and waited patiently. And, sure enough, at exactly 12 o'clock, they heard the knock. Instantly, Hal Morton flung open the door and Eleanor snapped on the flood lights in the yard. But as before, no one was there. There had certainly been no time for anyone to escape unseen, and yet the well-lighted yard was empty.

Who is it that raps at that door? The Mortons say they no longer want to know.

Hilda's House

Here is another haunting for which I can offer no satisfactory explanation. I am including it because I am personally well acquainted with Hilda and her family as well as with Cleo, the psychic in this story, and I believe them all to be sincere.

Perhaps some day someone will discover why Charles haunts and what it was that drew Hilda to him. Until then, this tale is to read, ponder, and enjoy.

Hilda was driving home from work. Headed west on Ford Road, she suddenly felt compelled to turn off her usual route and onto a small street named Argyle. Born in Dearborn, Hilda had lived most of her life there; but she had seldom, if ever, traveled Argyle Street. That day something gave her an inexplicable urge to do so. And there on Argyle was the house she felt was destined to be hers.

The small frame building looked much like all the others on that block, and Hilda was at a loss to explain why it mesmerized her. From then on, day after day, she went out of her way to turn down Argyle just to catch a glimpse of it.

Then one day a few months after she had first become fascinated by the house, a "For Sale" sign appeared on the front lawn. Hilda, who had had no thought of moving until that day, went directly home and called the realtor. Now wanting desperately to see the inside of the house, she made an appointment to visit it the next day.

As soon as she walked through the door, she felt that she had come home. Hilda felt it was where she belonged.

A single parent with a meager income, Hilda anticipated difficulty in raising the money for the down payment and qualifying for a mortgage. But to her surprise, this proved not so; everything fell into place as if it had been planned by a higher power. Before long, she and her children were happily settled in their new home.

Strangely, Hilda felt that she had somehow lived in the house before. She had never been so at peace, and the good feeling continued even after unusual things began to happen.

One evening while everyone was seated around the table at supper, there came strange tapping noises. They seemed to be coming from the floorboards beneath their feet, but there was no one in the basement. Thinking that the noises came from water pipes or some other readily explainable source, Hilda tried to make light of them and jokingly told her children that the house probably had a ghost. The words were hardly out of her mouth when the tapping became louder and more emphatic. It was an event that happened again and again.

One evening when guests were present, someone suggested working out a system of measured taps to enable Hilda to communicate with her unearthly housemate. The ghost cooperated; and through long, laborious questioning, the family came up with its name, "Charles." (A trip to City Hall soon disclosed that the very first owners of the house had been a couple named Charles and Mary Adams. They had moved in just after the house was built in 1929.)

For the next several years, the tapping would occur every now and then. And it became common to hear footsteps on the stairs when no one was there. Sometimes, the whole family would be awakened by the sound of furniture being moved about in the living room, although they later would find that everything was still as they had left it. This occurred on one occasion while Hilda's sister, Carol, was spending the night. Hilda told her not to worry — it was only Charles, and he was a friendly ghost.

But Carol didn't believe in ghosts and said that she wanted real proof of Charles. Immediately, a loud popping sound came from the electric clock as it spit sparks in all directions. It stopped dead at 4:25 a.m. and never worked again.

Relatives eventually convinced Hilda to have a medium conduct a seance to find out once and for all who this ghost really was and what he wanted. Hilda was reluctant because she was fond of Charles. She had never been afraid of him, and she feared a seance with strangers might frighten him away, which she didn't want. But she finally agreed to give it a try.

At the appointed hour, Cleo Abain (an internationally renowned psychic), Hilda, and six of her close friends and relatives gathered in the dining room of the house on Argyle Street. At first, all was quiet. Then suddenly, the room became filled with the strong smell of cigar smoke. The ghost they had conjured up was not that of Hilda's friend, Charles; instead it was that of a very angry, short, dark man who spoke of his daughter, Maria. He indicated he was looking for Charles Adams, whom he referred to as "Carlo." (Carlo is the Italian name for Charles, and while Charles Adams was not Italian, the man whose ghost was there that night appeared to be.)

Cleo Abain suggested that perhaps Maria had run away from home and died in the house while she had been a guest of the Adams family. Perhaps they had befriended her. As she toured the house, the psychic said that she felt strange vibrations in the basement. A great sadness came over her, and she suspected that at one time someone had committed suicide there. She also felt that a young woman and an older man (perhaps Maria and her father?) had once argued over a basset hound.

None of this was ever confirmed, but Hilda remained certain that Charles himself was not in any way connected with evil or foul play. She felt that he was a kind and understanding ghost, with deep sympathy for her problems. (I myself have wondered whether Hilda is the reincarnation of Maria or some other person whom Charles befriended in another lifetime.)

Charles' friendly spirit continued to comfort Hilda. Curiously, after the seance was held, the unpleasant odor of cigar smoke was also present on occasion.

Hilda no longer lives in her beloved home on Argyle Street. The main part of the house is now occupied by her son, a city police officer, and his wife and children. Hilda's daughter lives with a friend in an apartment in the basement.

To this very day, footsteps can still be heard on the stairs when no one is near them. Hilda's son has put a workbench in his garage and spends a great deal of time out there. He insists that Charles has never left and seems to like the new workshop, for his presence can be felt there as well as in the main house. He, like his mother, believes that Charles was a "good guy," and he rather enjoys having him around.

The Happy Ghost

Most ghosts seem to haunt because they are unhappy. But the one who lives in this beautiful old house in Saginaw, Michigan, is different. He is a happy ghost, for it seems he is finally realizing the dream of his lifetime.

My grandmother first told me this story when I was very young. My great-uncle, Edward Lickfeldt, worked with the George Rufner of this story on the Detroit and Mackinaw Railroad and they remained friends even after their fortunes took them on different roads. It was through Uncle Ed that George sought out my grandmother when he needed the advice of a witch.

George Rufner was from a poor family. His father had immigrated to this country from Germany, and his mother's people, who were farmers, came from the British Isles by way of Canada. George's mother's parents had been greatly opposed to their daughter marrying a "foreigner," even though they were only a generation removed from being immigrants themselves.

Martin Rufner, George's father, had worked hard at a number of different jobs, but never stayed in one place for very long. Always hoping to better his lot, he moved from one job to another. And try as he did, he was never able to purchase a real home for his family. They lived in one rented house after another, all in ill repair.

George's own life was not especially happy. His grandparents on his mother's side had never really forgiven their daughter for her marriage to an immigrant. If his father had any family left, they were still in Germany and he never spoke of them. Two of George's four siblings had died in infancy. His older sister had only lived to the age of nine and his younger brother had died at four. Both were victims of a diphtheria epidemic which had swept the country. George, too, had been ill with the disease at the same time but had miraculously survived.

During the years he was growing up, George attended school in at least five different communities. In spite of his family's misfortune, he was a good student and he loved to read. Whenever possible, he would visit libraries or borrow books from teachers or anyone else willing to lend them.

From early childhood on, George had harbored a secret dream. He wanted to live in a large stately home, a mansion with a huge staircase in the main hall and a back stairs for servants. He longed for a fireplace in every room, hand-carved woodwork, and molded plaster with designs on the ceilings. He was enthralled by stained glass windows and beveled glass doors. Such houses were described in great detail in the books he read. And one day when he was in the sixth grade, he actually visited one. His school friend, Andrew, had invited him to come home after school and stay for dinner. Andrew's father was an attorney, and the house they lived in had been built by a lumber baron a generation or so before.

George was in awe. At dinner, they sat at a long, highly polished mahogany table in the dining room. On it was fresh white linen, a far cry from the patterned oiled cloth never removed from the round table in the kitchen where his own family sat for meals. Dinner was served by a maid. And while George could never remember what he had eaten, he never forgot the bone china plates, stemmed crystal water goblets, and heavy sterling silver that graced the candlelit table that evening.

To George, the most impressive room in the house was the library. He loved the smell of the leather bound books on the shelves that lined the walls. He was intrigued by an ivory chess set on a small table beneath the French windows at the end of the room. He asked Andrew to teach him to play the game. Andrew refused. He told George that he didn't like the library; it was haunted, he said, by an old man who had once lived there. Andrew claimed that he had actually seen the ghost twice. George was thrilled. He had been fascinated by the many stories he had read about haunted houses. A ghost somehow made the house seem complete.

Although George had wanted to finish school, at 14 he was forced to quit and go to work when his father died. He was hired by the Detroit and Mackinaw Railroad where he continued to work for many years. Despite his enjoyment of the company of young ladies, he didn't marry, determined not to be saddled with supporting a family and trapped like his father in back-breaking poverty. Instead, he remained with his mother, caring for her until she died. George, still in his early twenties, then moved into a room in a boarding house. With few close friends and no relatives, his time was spent working or reading. What pleasure there was in his life came, as always, from books.

The years passed, and George saved all the money he could from his meager wages. Although he probably could have bought a small house, he chose not to. The only kind of house he really wanted to own was utterly beyond his reach, a fact that only served to intensify his fantasy. He would daydream for hours about the home he would own when he became rich. But he never really believed that would ever happen.

One day at work, George was called to leave the railroad yard and go to the office. It was the middle of the day. He had no family that might need him, he owed no one any money, he wasn't mixed up in anything illegal, and he certainly didn't qualify for a promotion. A request for his presence could only mean that his job was being terminated. That hardly proved to be the case. Waiting for him in the D&M Railroad office that day was a lawyer with a message that was to change his life.

Unbeknownst to George, his father, Martin Rufner, had been the only son of a very wealthy German family. As a young man, Martin had quarreled bitterly with his father and run away to the United States. Now a relative in Europe whom George had neither met nor even knew of, had died and left him an enormous sum of money. Even after both countries had collected their due taxes and the lawyers had been paid, there was still enough left for George to live out the rest of his life in the style he so fervently dreamed about.

George began at once to search for the house of his dreams. He traveled from Alpena to Port Huron looking for it. In Saginaw, he finally found it.

Built in the late 1800s, it was constructed completely of Michigan timber. Three stories high, with 15 rooms plus servants' quarters, it was almost exactly the way he had pictured it. The original owner had long since died. His son, having lost money in unwise investments, had allowed the house to fall into disrepair. This did not discourage George who looked forward to the challenge of restoring the house to its original splendor. He converted a bedroom on the first floor into a library. Paneling and lumber from another house of the same period were purchased to line the walls and build the bookshelves. He kept workmen busy for weeks repairing plaster, refinishing floors, cleaning chimneys, and putting all the fireplaces into working order. He attended auctions and estate sales in search of the perfect furniture for each room. He chose paintings and accessories to create the elegant atmosphere he sought. Traveling to the eastern states, he purchased volumes of old books to fill his library, where he had already placed an enormous highly-polished desk, a large leather chair, and a small table displaying a hand-carved chess set.

He hired a woman named Mable Easter to keep house for him and taught her exactly how he wanted things done.

Even when dining alone, he ate all of his meals in the formal dining room. Dinner was always served by candlelight on fine table linen, with exquisite china, crystal, and silver.

George made an effort to cultivate new friendships with people he deemed worthy of visiting his home. He entertained at small intimate dinner parties, mainly to show off his beloved house. Although lacking in formal education, George was extremely well read and could converse intelligently with far more learned people. His small circle of new acquaintances came to respect him and enjoy his company. He, in turn, was often invited into their homes, where he carefully observed their possessions and lifestyles, comparing them with his own.

By that time, George should have been very happy. To a certain extent, he was. But even when his house was completed to perfection, with every room ready to be enjoyed, there was an emptiness he couldn't define. He had all the friends he wanted and, even though he could now afford a wife and children, he knew he didn't fancy that idea at all.

It finally dawned on him. The house needed a ghost.

All his life, the house he had imagined had been haunted by the friendly spirit of some former resident. This house needed a spectral presence, something money would not buy. George began to seriously research ghosts. He traveled the country visiting places that were said to be haunted. He read every authoritative book written on hauntings. He even went so far as to consult with a witch (my own grandmother) about trying to conjure up a spirit to dwell in his home. The wise woman warned him that a spirit called up in that way was more likely to be an angry one, evil and malignant, than the benign friendly sort he had in mind!

In spite of the lack of a ghost, George enjoyed his fine home for several years. He played chess with his friends and even entertained a special lady friend who had come into his life. But he would often sit for hours in his beloved library bemoaning the house's imperfection. And then he struck upon an idea. He was growing old, and he knew he would not live more than another few years at the most. He loved his beautiful home and didn't want to leave it, so why not spend eternity there?

George decided that he would die and haunt the house himself.

People began to notice a remarkable change in George. He was always smiling or humming a happy little tune under his breath. It was as if he knew a very pleasant secret.

He met with his lawyer and drew up a will, leaving his home and all its treasures to Mable Easter, his housekeeper. He also left her adequate money for its upkeep and explicit directions for keeping it exactly the way he liked it. When everything was in order, George went into the library, closed the door, and shot himself in the head.

Mable Easter lived on in the house for another ten years until she became too senile to care for it or for herself. After she left the house, legal technicalities kept it empty for several years. Then a doctor purchased the property and repaired the damage done by neglect. Since that time, several families have occupied George's home. All of them claim that the library is haunted.

But the library ghost is not a frightening one. It is often heard humming a cheerful tune. Some claim to have seen it. They describe a pleasant looking old fellow who is usually reading a book or studying the chess board. He wears a satisfied smile and never seems to notice them at all.

XI

Exorcism

Exorcism as a way of getting rid of ghosts is greatly overrated. I'm sorry to say that there is no ritual that will drive away a spirit. You can tell a ghost to leave and it usually will at the time. But unless you find out why it haunts and help it solve its problem, it will return sooner or later.

There is one kind of haunting, however, that can usually be eliminated with a rather simple ceremony. This is a situation in which a ghost haunts not because it has a message to impart, but because it simply doesn't know it's dead.

I've included this story because I played a part in helping a troubled spirit find some peace.

Show Me the Way to Go Home

Jed and Sarah Taylor had lived for more than 40 years in their two-story frame house on a quiet street in Ann Arbor. Jed himself had built the addition on the house, adding two bedrooms as their family had grown. The children grew up, married, and established homes of their own. Soon, Jed and Sara had grandchildren and even great-grandchildren who visited often and filled the house with love and laughter.

But things began to change. Jed developed terminal lung cancer and sadness hung over the once happy home. Sara was getting older and her health was not as good as it once had been. It became ever harder for her to take care of her husband. Feeding him, bathing him, and turning him in his bed soon became more than she could handle.

It was decided that Jed would go to live in a nursing home during his last days. But Jed resisted, and begged to be allowed to die at home. But it was impossible and he was soon moved to a suitable establishment near his daughter's home. Not wanting to stay in the house without him, Sara closed it up and went to live with their daughter.

Since Sara knew she would probably never live there again, she instructed their oldest son, who was handling their financial affairs, to sell the house as soon as possible. And so it was that while Jed was still lying in the nursing home begging to be taken back to his own house, Donald and Elaine Parker purchased the house and happily moved into it with their 18-month-old son.

The Parkers had been in the house almost a month when Elaine took the baby and went shopping with her nextdoor neighbor. When the two women returned home, they looked up at an upstairs window and saw what appeared to be an old man wearing pajamas and a bath robe.

"My land," exclaimed the neighbor, "I swear that's old Jed Taylor. What's he doing in your house?"

"I don't know," answered Elaine, "but let's find out right now."

They unlocked the door, went inside, and searched the house upstairs and down. They found no sign of anyone anywhere.

Elaine told Donald about it that evening, explaining that both she and the neighbor had clearly seen the old man in the upstairs window. But he laughed and said they had been seeing things. He said that perhaps the sun shining on the house across the road was reflected in the window, causing an optical illusion. Elaine said no more about it and the incident was forgotten. Until the weekend.

On Saturday, Donald's brother David came over and asked if he might borrow some of Donald's tools. Donald told him to go down to the workbench in the basement and help himself. At the foot of the stairs, David came face-to-face with an old man dressed in pajamas, robe, and slippers. He was startled, for his brother had not told him anyone was there.

"What do you want?" asked the elderly gentleman.

"I came to get some of my brother's tools," answered David.

"Take them all," said the older man, "they don't belong here anyway."

David took what he wanted and went back upstairs. "Who's the old guy in the basement?" he asked his brother.

"What old guy? There's no one down there," replied Donald.

"Yes, there is," said David. "I was just talking to him."

Both men went downstairs. There was no one there, but when David described the visitor, he sounded like the same person Elaine had seen in the window. Donald could perhaps dismiss one such incident as a figment of the imagination. But not two. Clearly, the old fellow had run away from the nursing home and was hiding somewhere on the premises. After all, he had built part of the house and had lived there for more than 40 years. He most likely knew of some crawl space the Parkers had not discovered yet. The thing to do, of course, was call Mr. Taylor's daughter and tell her that her father had returned to his old house.

The daughter answered the phone, listened carefully to Donald, and then said sadly, "I'm sorry, Mr. Parker, but you must be mistaken. My father died almost a week ago."

But old Jed Taylor continued to make his presence felt. One day while Donald was at work and the baby was napping, Elaine decided to relax in a hot bath. She left the bathroom door ajar so that she might hear her baby if he woke up. Suddenly, there was Jed, admonishing her for having no modesty: "Young lady, if you must bathe in my house, at least have the decency to close the bathroom door." After that, Elaine determined that either Jed would have to go or they would move out. Donald agreed. And, since they were Catholics they approached their parish priest with the problem.

The priest visited the home and talked with everyone who had seen the ghost of old Jed Taylor. Though convinced that what they said was true, he could not perform an exorcism of Jed's spirit without the consent of the Bishop. The Bishop did not believe the house was haunted and would not grant such permission.

At that point, the Parkers and their priest asked me to help with their dilemma. It was clear that Jed Taylor was not an evil spirit; he meant no harm to anyone. But he had died unhappily, wanting desperately to return to his beloved home. When his spirit was released from his body by death, it went to the place where he had been happy.

A simple ceremony was performed to convince Jed that he was dead and free to leave worldly things to the earthbound and go on to what would come next. Later, the parish priest blessed the house and masses were said at the Parker's church for Jed's soul.

Since then, all has been peaceful in the little house in Ann Arbor, and Jed Taylor has not been seen again.

XII

Seances

People often ask me how to hold a seance. There are several different types of seances. The most common, the one often seen in old movies, involves a professional medium who sits with the other participants and receives messages for them from spirits or spirit guides. I am not suggesting that all professional mediums are phonies, but you surely can see the possibilities such a drama might offer to a person inclined to trickery. Many intelligent but grief stricken and lonely people have been taken in by these so-called mediums. Here is an example from my family.

My great uncle and aunt were married for many years and had successfully raised ten children. In June, my uncle was going to retire and he and his wife would then be free to do all the wonderful things they had planned and saved for all of their lives. But in January my aunt died.

That summer, wretchedly unhappy with his new solitary life, Uncle Ed answered an ad in the Bay City Times and went to see a medium. After several attempts to contact his dead wife, my uncle believed she finally materialized at a seance conducted by the woman. This success encouraged him to return again and again to the medium. Finally, during one of these sessions, the medium told Uncle Ed that his wife would not come back any more and that she was now releasing him from his wedding vows. The deceased wife, said the medium, had said it was not good for a man to be alone and he should marry again. When Uncle Ed said that he knew of no one to marry, the ghost of his dead wife allegedly suggested the medium.

They got married, but did not live happily ever after. Six weeks later, Uncle Ed's new wife disappeared along with his life's savings.

◆ ◆ ◆

If you wish to hold a seance with a professional medium, do it with an open mind as an interesting experiment. But do not believe all you think you see and hear. Pay one price (for the entertainment), and leave your checkbook and the rest of your money at home.

In Chapter V, about poltergeists, I described what I call a pseudo (or make believe) seance. Lots of energy was worked up in that event but the people involved were experiencing poltergeist activity. In a seance, this is more likely than reaching a ghost. I don't believe you can simply sit down and page any old ghost you want and get results. (I hope I'm right. I'd hate to think that after I die anyone who wants to can call me back to make their party interesting!) I believe that a well-adjusted ghost is not hanging around waiting to attend your party. However, if there is one who might have reason to contact you, you might just be able to help it along by making the conditions more favorable.

For a real seance, the room should be set up in much the same way as described in Chapter V, although some groups dispense with a table and simply seat themselves in a circle, holding hands. The lights should be dimmed and, instead of concentrating on the table, movement, or energies, the participants should simply sit quietly, perhaps chanting or singing softly in unison. This sometimes seems to produce a hypnotic effect and people often drift into a trance-like state. While in this state, many say they receive what they believe to be messages from the dead. Others may only be bringing forth things from the deep recesses of their own minds. Unfortunately, I know of no way to prove which is which; you must decide for yourself.

Here are some suggestions for making your seance a success:

1. Make sure that all those participating in the experiment are open-minded, if not actual believers. One non-believer can prevent the group from setting up the right vibrations, and a joker or prankster can simply upset the whole procedure.

2. No one who is in less than full control of his or her senses should play with this, or with any other psychic phenomenon. If you drink, take any kind of drug or tonic, even if prescribed by a doctor, or if you are emotionally unstable or

overly excitable, I suggest that you sit the seance out. It is not for you.

3. Prepare the room well in advance. It should be well ventilated and neither too warm nor too cold. It often helps to burn a spiritual incense — frankincense or High John — in the room about an hour before the sitting begins.

4. There are several ways to form your circle. Sitting around a table is only one way. My favorite is for the seekers to form their circle seated comfortably in straight-backed chairs and holding hands. Another way is to have the members of the group lie on the floor, holding hands, with their heads to the center of the circle and their feet to the outer edge of it.

5. The lighting should be very dim, but the room should not be totally dark. Candlelight does nicely. Many modern homes have lights with dimmer switches that are excellent for achieving just the right amount of light.

6. When your circle is formed, it helps to practice some simple breathing exercises to help each person relax and prepare for full participation. This also establishes a group rhythm. Try breathing in four counts, holding your breath for four counts, and exhaling for four counts. Count: In, 2, 3, 4; Hold, 2, 3, 4; and Out, 2, 3, 4. Repeat this at least nine times.

7. Chanting or singing softly also seems to enhance the mood and bring on paranormal phenomena. One chant you can use for this purpose is: "Ta ma, Am ma, A lee ta." Chant it in unison softly and slowly.

8. I would not suggest more than a 45-minute sitting for a beginning group. Set a timer before you begin your seance and, when it signals, the group should again go into their breathing exercises to bring them slowly back to the here-and-now.

9. Do not be alarmed if one of your members remains in a trance-like state. Turn up the lights and talk normally. Offer the person some water and allow him or her to rest. I have a registered nurse (and smelling salts) present at all of the seances I conduct. I do this mainly because I do not always know all of the people in the circle well and it seems to make everyone feel safer and more relaxed.

Here is a story about an attempted seance.

The Case of the Shattered Mirror

Larry Smallwood and his family were enchanted with the large old woodframe house that stood on a tree-lined street in the downriver community of Wyandotte. It featured high ceilings, alcoves, and nooks and crannies not to be found in more recently-built homes. The house had been empty for some time and was in need of repair. But the price was right, and all agreed it was the house for them.

The Smallwoods enjoyed redecorating the comfortable old place, and it wasn't long before they were settled in. There were four large bedrooms and for the first time in their lives, each of the three children, all teenagers, had a separate bedroom. Larry and his wife, Joan, were delighted with the woodburning fireplace in the master bedroom and looked forward to spending many restful and romantic evenings there.

From the moment the Smallwoods moved in, they all had heard strange noises in the house from time to time. At first, they were not alarmed and attributed the sounds to the old building settling or to other natural phenomena. But before long, they began to confess to each other that they sometimes felt the presence of someone or something in the house with them. They all started to wonder whether the house might be haunted.

One cold dark January night, about six months after they had moved in, Larry suggested that it might be worthwhile to hold a seance. All the lights were turned out, and the room was lit only by a street light shining in through the window. They seated themselves around the table in the dining room.

On one side of the room stood a beautiful old buffet, and above it hung a large decorative mirror that had come with the house when they purchased it. Larry was seated at the head of the table with his back to the mirror. Joan was seated opposite him, facing the mirror, and the children sat between them on each side of the table. Clutching hands, they sat quietly for half an hour. (Larry now admits that he almost dozed off from boredom, since it seemed that nothing at all was going to happen.) Suddenly, there was a flash of blue light. Then came the sounds of babbling voices and then breaking glass as the huge mirror on the wall above the buffet shattered and fell.

Everyone screamed in fright and the circle was immediately broken. Joan jumped up and turned on the lights.

Larry himself was badly shaken, but the others were even more upset, for they had seen something he had not. The image of a young man wearing a sailor's uniform had clearly appeared in the mirror just before it had shattered. Larry, his back to the mirror, could not see it.

Later, questioning the neighbors, the Smallwoods learned that the last person to live in the house had been an elderly widow whose only son had been lost at sea in World War II. They described her as "a bit balmy" since she went about the house talking to herself, claiming to be holding a conversation with her long dead son. After her death, the house had stood empty until they purchased it.

The Smallwoods continued to live on in the house for several years. But after the night of the seance, they did not experience any more ghostly visits.

XIII

Four Favorite Tales

I'll close this collection with four of my own personal favorites. These are tales whose sites I've actually visited, or whose central figures were especially intriguing to me.

Chapman's Chair at Silver Creek

It was a cold, wet Saturday in late September, 1980. Don McGregor, a former fellow teacher who was by then the principal of Mark Wegienka Elementary School in Woodhaven, had invited me to go for a walk with him. Don had learned that I was collecting ghost stories and had called to say that he had a good one for me, one he had first come upon 20 years earlier. He offered to take me to the site of the story, along the banks of Silver Creek.

The persistent rain the day we went had made the riverbank very slippery and I lost my footing. Falling down in the mud, I slid down the slope like an otter and ended up sitting in the shallow water looking, I'm sure, like a drowned rat. Mud dripped off my nose, but the only thing hurt was my dignity. Don helped me to my feet and we waded the rest of the way across the creek. As we walked along, he told this story.

In southern Wayne County, Woodruff Road runs westward from Jefferson Avenue through the small community of Rockwood to the town of Flat Rock. It had originated as a track for early wagon drivers so they could avoid the swampy area closer to the Huron River. It still roughly follows the course of Silver Creek, a smaller stream that empties into the river.

In 1961, Don had been walking along the wooded banks of the creek when, just across the creek in the middle of nowhere, he saw a weatherbeaten old chair sitting on top of a cement platform. He waded across the creek to get a better look at it and discovered that the hand-carved chair was actually chained and bolted in place. His curiosity aroused, he began to question the local residents.

It seemed that the parcel of land that lies between Woodruff Road and Silver Creak was originally owned by an Austin Chapman. In his later years, Austin, who lived to be 80, enjoyed nothing more than sitting for hours by the creek fishing or just watching the nearby birds and small animals. He had built a wooden chair for himself and placed it on the bank of the stream, where the view was best. He had told his family never, even after his death, to move the chair for, if such things were possible, he would return from his grave to sit on it from time to time and enjoy the beauty and tranquility of the spot he loved so dearly.

Sometime after his death in 1931, the property had been sold to Hosse Devers, who built his house on the other side of Woodruff Road, away from the creek. He parceled off the land and sold the portion on the creek to Father Parquette, a Catholic priest from Monroe. In 1954, the priest built a house there where he lived with his housekeeper, a Mrs. Bannister, and her invalid son. Although the house stood well back from the road, it was still a good distance from the water which could not be seen from it.

As soon as they moved into the newly-built home, Father Parquette and Mrs. Bannister were greatly troubled by what the priest believed to be a poltergeist. Strange noises could be heard at all hours of the day and night. Things were tossed about and dishes were broken. The electricity worked only half the time and when it did, lights would flicker on and off for no particular reason. Electricians were called. The power would always work well while they were there; but as soon as they left, everything would go haywire again.

When a formal Catholic exorcism ceremony and house blessing failed to change anything, Father Parquette went to visit two of Mr. Chapman's grandsons, Almond and Delmont, to ask if their family had ever experienced any strange phenomena on the property. One of them remembered the chair and asked whether it had been disturbed. The priest said he recalled finding an old chair when he was clearing the underbrush near the creek. He had tossed it onto a pile of old branches and shrubs.

It was suggested that perhaps Austin Chapman's ghost might be angry about that.

Willing to try anything, the good Father hastened to find the chair. He repaired it, waterproofed it, and returned it to its original spot beside the creek. The troubles that had been disturbing his household then ceased completely. And, to make certain that no one ever disturbed the chair again, he built a cement platform and chained and bolted the chair in place upon it.

When we visited the place that day in 1980, we found that the elements had destroyed the chair and floods had washed away the wood. But the cement platform remained to attest to Austin Chapman's right to sit there.

The priest, his housekeeper, and her son had all passed away by that time, and in 1972 the Gorst family purchased the property. They never experienced anything unusual there. But then, they never disturbed the spot by the creek Austin Chapman had reserved for himself so long ago.

Garage Sale Ghost

The national pastime in this country has always been baseball. But these days, although I have no statistics to prove it, I think perhaps that's changing to garage-saling. Everyone, regardless of finances, seems to enjoy the weekend bargain hunt. Of course, it must be called an "estate sale" before some people will venture forth. Whatever it's called, it's fun to rummage through someone else's discards. One man's junk is, indeed, another man's treasure.

The two young ladies in this story furnished their apartment with garage sale goodies. But they soon found out they had gotten more than they had bargained for.

Gerri and Donna were good friends. They had met through their work as lab technicians in the research department of one of the major automotive companies. Both were intelligent, well-educated, young, attractive, and single. Each was still living at home with her parents and anxious to get out on her own.

In order to save money, the girls decided to share an apartment. Luckily, they found a two-story townhouse in Southfield in their price range. But after paying the first and last months' rent, and a security deposit, they had very little money left to outfit their new home. So, for the first few weeks, they slept on mattresses on the bedroom floors and ate their meals at a card table set up in the kitchen. Their only chairs were folding chairs donated by Gerri's mother. But they were happy. They even cooked fancy dinners for their boyfriends.

Every payday the two friends answered newspaper ads for used furniture they could afford and before long they had made the apartment attractive and comfortable. The vacuum cleaner, TV, and most of their dishes came from garage sales. One Saturday at an estate sale in Birmingham, Donna fell in love with an old trunk which the owner said her grandmother had brought from Germany more than a century earlier. She was asking a high price for it, but it was quite unusual and in excellent condition. After haggling awhile, she and Donna came to terms and the price was reduced. Donna loaded her purchase into the back of her Bronco and headed home, delighted with the newly-acquired treasure.

While cleaning and refinishing the trunk, Donna decided to reline it as well. Removing the old lining, she discovered a small

secret compartment inside the curved top. Inside it was an exquisite-
ly crafted antique jewelry box containing a gold ring with a green
stone and a matching necklace. While she showed her discovery to
Gerri, both girls experienced the strange feeling that they were not
alone in the room.

Donna took the jewelry case upstairs to her bedroom and put it
on her dresser. When she returned later to her room for the night, she
found her bed rumpled as if someone had been lying on it.

Soon, the girls began to hear scratching noises in the walls. They
thought they had mice, so Gerri's boyfriend gave them a cat. But the
cat hissed and blew at nothing at all. After a few hours, it ran away
and was never seen again. The scratching noises continued, so the
girls set traps; they never caught a single mouse.

One day when she was home alone, Gerri heard a woman crying
in the bedroom upstairs. Assuming that Donna had come home, she
went upstairs to see what was wrong. A woman in a long dress was
standing before the open jewel box in Donna's room holding the
green necklace. She was crying pitifully. Gerri was not frightened.
The intruder seemed so sad and so in need of comfort.

"Hello," said Gerri. "What's wrong? Can I help you?"

The woman looked directly at her and then vanished before her
eyes, leaving the old necklace lying on the floor. Gerri rushed downstairs and out the door. She walked about a bit. Surely her mind was
playing tricks on her? She couldn't have seen a ghost — not in a
brand new modern building in a city like Southfield. Slowly she
regained her composure and returned home, but decided not to tell
Donna about the incident.

That night, both girls were awakened by banging noises in the
apartment and got up to investigate. They found nothing disturbed
and soon returned to bed. In the weeks that followed, the scratching
in the walls continued and the banging noises were heard again by
both girls and by Donna's mother who had come for a visit.

One weekend, Gerri went out of town with friends. Donna invited her boyfriend over for the evening. They had a romantic candlelit
dinner, and he stayed very late. After he left, Donna cleaned up the
kitchen and went upstairs to bed. It was nearly 4 a.m. Lying in bed
trying to sleep, she heard a noise. It sounded as if someone else were
in the room. She sat up, and by the faint light coming through the
window curtain, she saw a figure standing in front of her dresser.

Terrified, Donna watched as the figure opened her jewelry box.

Summoning all her courage, she decided to confront the burglar. Reaching over to the bedside, she snapped on the light. To her shock, the intruder was a woman wearing a long black dress. She looked sadly into Donna's eyes and then vanished.

The next morning, Donna found the ring with the green stone lying at the foot of the stairs.

Many violent thunderstorms that summer caused a great deal of damage in Oakland County where the girls lived. One night, frightened by yet another storm and edgy about what they had seen in Donna's bedroom (for by now, they had shared their weird experiences), the two girls decided to sleep downstairs on the living room floor. In the midst of the storm, the electricity went off. Soon they heard bumping and rustling sounds in the room. Telling themselves it was only the wind blowing things about, they got up and rechecked all the windows they had already closed because of the rain. The next morning, they discovered that the old trunk Donna was so proud of had been opened in the night (certainly not by the wind), and the books and papers stored inside were scattered about.

The following weekend, the girls took the trunk, jewel case, and jewelry to an antique dealer. They didn't tell him the real reason they wanted to sell those items, only that they needed as much cash as they could get for them.

Although Donna made a hefty profit, she doesn't think she'll be shopping at any more garage sales.

Things are quiet in the girls' townhouse now. The scratching and bumping noises have stopped altogether, and they have had no more visits from their sad-eyed ghostly intruder. But Gerri and Donna are hardly bored by the new calm. In fact, they rather like it that way.

Fishing Buddies

Although the events in this story occurred in Florida, all of the characters in it, including the ghost, were originally from Michigan.

Although Jim Mullins lived in Michigan, he was never fond of winters in the Great Lakes Region. Each year, for several weeks, he would visit his friend, Red the Clown, in Sarasota. Red, too, was originally from Michigan as was his next door neighbor, Murray, who had moved to Florida when he retired.

Red had never really cared much for fishing, but Jim and Murray loved it, and over the years, the two had become great fishing buddies. They would spend hours sitting together on the seawall in front of Red's house fishing for snapper, ocean trout, or whatever else they could catch.

Jim also enjoyed snorkeling and although Murray wasn't a swimmer, he would watch Jim and declare that some day he was going to try it "for sure" himself.

Although the two men enjoyed each other's company every winter, they never corresponded in between times.

One year as usual, Red invited Jim to come down South and enjoy the sunshine. When he arrived in Sarasota after driving all the way from Michigan with very little sleep, Jim was tired and anxious to get into the house and unpack. But when he drove into the driveway, he saw Murray out in his yard and stopped to talk with him. He showed Murray his new fishing rod and promised to fish with him the next day. Murray asked him if he planned on going snorkeling again. When Jim said "Yes," Murray said that if he didn't get up the courage to try it himself, he would at least enjoy watching Jim. The two men then parted, promising to meet the next morning at their regular fishing spot.

Jim carried his gear into the house and was warmly greeted by Red who said, "I heard you drive up quite a while ago. What took you so long to come inside?" Jim explained that he had stopped to chat for a while with Murray.

Red looked at him in disbelief. "You didn't talk to Murray," he said.

"Yes, I did," replied Jim. "He said he'd been waiting for me to arrive."

"You couldn't have talked to Murray," said Red sadly. "Murray went on a vacation to Key West and was hit by a truck while crossing the street. He's been dead for nearly nine months."

The Ghost of Minnie Quay

I've saved the best until last. This is my all time favorite ghost story.

I first heard of Minnie Quay in 1980 while on a camping trip to Lake Huron. I wrote up a brief account of her story as the camp caretaker had told it to us and filed it away for future use. Seven years later, I wrote a Halloween article for the Detroit Free Press *about haunted places to visit in Michigan, and I included the information I had about Minnie. The day after the story appeared, I received a phone call from Bill Clugston, who then owned a tavern called the Forester Inn. He told me that I had not only misspelled Minnie's name, I'd mistakenly said the events had taken place in Port Sanilac in the early 1900s. In fact, they occurred four miles north of there in Forester, Michigan, in the 1870s. Bill said that if I wanted to know more about Minnie, I should come to Forester. (Through Bill, I later met Jim and Debbie Thompson, the new owners of the Quay family home. They invited me to visit the house and spend the night there.)*

The day after Bill's call, I drove with a friend 150 miles to the little community of Forester in the Michigan thumb. And within the next 24 hours, I was walking on a Lake Huron beach at midnight with a group of people I didn't know, in search of Minnie's ghost. I had thus embarked on what was to become one of the most interesting adventures of my life.

It was my good fortune to later meet several descendants of Minnie's sister Amanda, some of whom have given hours of their time helping me research the story of the unfortunate young girl who lived and died in Forester, Michigan, more than 100 years ago.

I hope the story I present to you here will whet your appetite. Since writing it, I have spent four more years in search of the details of Minnie's story, and have come across additional information that leads me to believe that perhaps she did not take her own life after all, although her death certificate records a suicide. I am now writing a book about the ghost of Minnie Quay. Until it is finished, I offer you the following.

It was August, 1980. Our family and a group of friends had rented cottages together on the shores of Lake Huron two miles south of Forester, Michigan. Arriving on a Saturday morning, we did all the things that campers usually do — played games, hiked, swam, enjoyed the beach, and cooked meals over an open fire. Around the campfire that night we sang, talked, and eventually began telling the inevitable ghost stories.

One of the men in the group had planned a little surprise. He

slipped away unnoticed and donned a gorilla costume he had secret-
ly brought. He then circled wide around the cabins, cut through the
woods, and emerged from the trees on the other side of the campfire
during the spookiest part of one of the ghost stories. One woman
saw him and let out a piercing scream that threw even the bravest
members of the group into a state of fright. The huge hairy beast
lumbered toward us through the shadowy darkness and into the
flickering firelight. Then in a flash, the prankster unmasked and
everyone relaxed, declaring of course that they had known of the
prank all along.

But we all huddled a bit closer together after that, and those who
had planned to sleep on the beach opted instead for their cabins,
claiming they thought it might rain.

As the evening wore on, we imagined several times that we saw
the figure of a woman dressed in white, walking along the beach and
moving among the trees. Around midnight, the fire died down and
everyone went to bed.

Then suddenly at 3 a.m., four teenage girls who were sharing a
cabin ran screaming to their parents' cottages, certain that they'd
heard someone crying outside their back window. Carrying flash-
lights, we searched carefully around the cottages but found no one.
At last, we returned to bed to sleep fitfully for the rest of the night to
the sounds of the wind moaning in the trees and the waves lapping
the shore.

On Sunday morning, the camp's caretaker stopped by to check
on us. When we assured him all was well, he seemed relieved and
said, "Then Minnie didn't bother you after all?" When asked what
he meant, he told us the story of a young woman named Minnie
Quay who many years earlier had lived just north of the campsite in
Forester.

It seems that this poor girl had fallen in love with a sailor who
had lost his life at sea when his ship went down in a storm. Broken-
hearted, she reportedly took her own life by walking off the town
pier. He explained that since her drowning many people claimed to
have seen Minnie's ghost walking on the beach or among the trees
along the shore. Over the years, several young women had reported
that Minnie had beckoned them into the water, and the caretaker
declared that at least one girl had drowned following her gesture. He
also told us that the campers in the next group of cabins said they
had seen Minnie walking the shore the night before and had even

heard her crying mournfully. None of us would admit to taking him seriously, and we all accused the prankster with the ape suit of making up the Minnie Quay story and bribing the caretaker to come by and tell it to us. But this proved untrue. I became quite interested in Minnie's story and came back to the area later to question residents about it.

On M-25, four miles north of Port Sanilac along the shore of Lake Huron, stands a clump of buildings. They are all that remains of the original, once-thriving lumbering town of Forester, Michigan. Technically, Forester doesn't exist since it was never incorporated as a city, a village, or a township. But its campgrounds and cabins are filled to capacity during the summer months. Year-round residents number less than 40. Boarded up buildings that once housed a post office, a general store, and a pharmacy attest to livelier times gone by. The 150-year-old Tanner House, a 22-room hotel that thrived in the lumbering days (and was later used as a gambling house, a blind pig, and a house of prostitution,) now stands empty, a specter of the past. A country tavern (Bill Clugston's Forester Inn), a small gift shop, and an antique store that keeps very irregular hours are the only places still doing business there.

Across the road from the tavern stands an impressive blue two-story house with the year "1852" and the name "Quay" lettered above the door. Its present owners, Jim and Debbie Johnson, plan to repair and restore it for use as a bed-and-breakfast.

But Forester is a ghost town in more than one sense, for it is believed by many to be haunted by the spirit of the young woman known as Minnie Quay.

James Quay and his wife, Mary Ann, had come to Forester from New England. Their daughter, Minnie, was the second oldest of their seven children. The eldest daughter, Lulu, had died at the age of nine, leaving Minnie the oldest child and big sister to the remaining five children. Had she lived until May 29, 1876, she would have been 15 years old, but Minnie died on April 26.

At that time, Forester was a busy lumbering town with a population of close to 400. There were four large warehouses along the shore and a pier that extended far out into the bay. (The pilings of the old pier can still be seen there today.) Large freighters as well as passenger ships pulled into the Forester pier. Most of these ships were sailing vessels, but steam-powered ships had begun to become more popular each year. Whenever a ship docked, the townspeople would rush down to the pier for news from the outside world. Old men sat, day in and day out, on the porch of the Tanner House, watching the waterfront activities. When the ships dropped anchor, the seamen — some of them barely in their teens — would come ashore.

Minnie Quay, like many other girls of her day, gave her heart to one of these young men. No one knows for sure what his name was, or even the name of the ship he sailed on. But it is not hard to picture him, young and strong, perhaps a bit arrogant. To young Minnie, he must have seemed worldly-wise when he talked of visiting such far-away places as Detroit, Chicago, and Sault St. Marie.

In a small town like Forester, it didn't take long for word to get back to the older Quays that their daughter Minnie was cavorting with a sailor. It was even rumored that she had become pregnant. This was later proven untrue, but her parents certainly could not be blamed for their concern about their young daughter's romance. Legend says that they forbade her ever to see her young swain again. Her mother was said to be so upset that she shouted, loudly enough for passers-by to hear, "I would rather see you dead, Minnie Quay, than married to a no-good sailor."

Then, in the early spring of 1876, word reached Minnie that her true love had been lost at sea in a treacherous storm. It was more than she could bear, especially since her parents had not allowed her to say goodbye when he had left Forester that last time.

A few days later, poor unhappy Minnie was left at home to take care of her baby brother, Charles. The other four children climbed into the horse-drawn buggy and accompanied their parents on an all-day trip to Port Sanilac, four miles south of Forester. Late in the afternoon, just before her parents were expected to return, Minnie left the baby sleeping peacefully at home and walked down to the pier. As she passed the Tanner House, she waved to the people sitting on the veranda. They waved back, and then watched her as she walked to the end of the pier. The next thing they knew she had plunged to her death in the cold, cold waters of Lake Huron, joining her lost beloved.

But it seems that since then fate has been unkind and the star-crossed pair have never been reunited. Although Minnie was buried in the Forester Cemetery at the north end of town, her soul still does not rest in peace. Her unhappy ghost, bound forever to Forester where she lived her short, sad life, still roams the shore crying out in vain as she searches for her long lost love.

An old folk song, "The Balled of Minnie Quay," has been popular in the Forester area for more than 100 years. Passed down from generation to generation, no one knows its origin. As time has gone by, several variations have developed. Here is the one I like best:

The Ballad of Minnie Quay

1

'Twas long ago beside Lake Huron
She walked the sandy shore.
But the voice of one sweet Minnie Quay
'Twill echo ever more.

2

Sailors still hear her crying.
Young lovers hear her, too,
As she calls for them to join her
In the waters, icy blue.

3

Young Minnie loved a sailor.
The sailor loved her, too.
And on the shore, behind the trees
The pair would rendezvous.

4

But gossips soon got wind of it,
And tongues began to wag.
The tale was told to Minnie's Ma
By some old babbling hag.

5

Minnie's Ma got angry
And to her daughter said,
"Married to a sailor?
I'd rather see you dead."

6

They knew that she'd been sneaking out
To see the lad at night.
They boarded up her bedroom door,
And kept her locked in tight.

7

He waited for his love, in vain.
A tear was in his eye
When he set sail next morning
Without kissing her goodbye.

8

He never saw his love again
For alas, a storm arose.
That raging gale sank many ships,
And his was one of those.

9

They ship that carried Minnie's love
Sank like it was lead.
And when the news reached Forester
They said that he was dead.

10

Minnie wore a dress of white.
She looked just like a bride,
When she plunged into the water deep
To die there by his side.

11

But Minnie Quay is not at rest,
Or so the people say.
Her ghost still walks the lonely shore.
You may see her to this day.

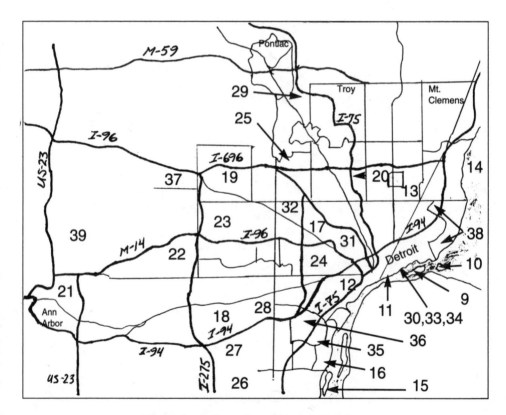

Detroit & Southeastern Michigan
(see key on page 128)

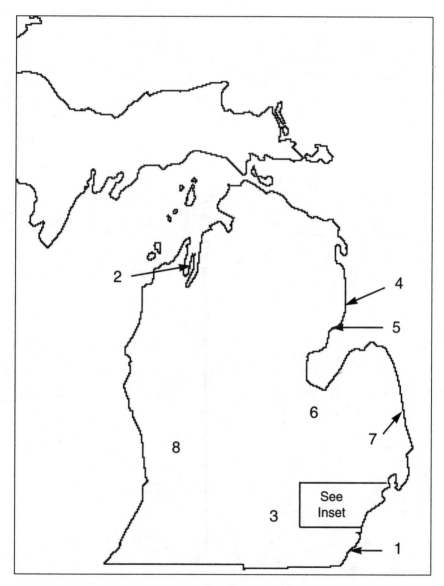

Michigan
(see key on page 128)